Meaning and Language

Meaning and Language

Satya Sundar Sethy

PRINTWORLD
Publishers of Indian Traditions

Cataloging in Publication Data — DK
[Courtesy: D.K. Agencies (P) Ltd. <docinfo@dkagencies.com>]

Sethy, Satya Sundar, 1981- author.
Meaning and language / Satya Sundar Sethy.
pages ; cm
Includes bibliographical references and index.
ISBN 9788124608548

1. Meaning (Philosophy) 2. Logical atomism. 3. Holism.
4. Language and languages — Philosophy. I. Title.

B105.M4S48 2016 DDC 121.68 23

ISBN 978-81-246-0854-8
First published in India in 2016

Printed and published by:
D.K. Printworld (P) Ltd.
Regd. Office: Vedaśrī, F-395, Sudarshan Park
(Metro Station: Ramesh Nagar), New Delhi - 110 015
Phones: (011) 2545 3975, 2546 6019; *Fax*: (011) 2546 5926
e-mail: indology@dkprintworld.com
Website: www.dkprintworld.com

To

my mother

Sukanti Sethy

Preface

THE MAIN objective of the inquiry undertaken in this study is to explore the nature of meaning and the way it functions in language. Investigation of meaning is not a recent concern in philosophy. Philosophers traditionally were interested in the question of meaning. This is evident from the work of philosophers such as Aristotle, Aquinas, Locke, Kant and Hume. But their interest in the study of meaning was not central to philosophical inquiry. However, contemporary philosophy takes a radical turn. It is a turn towards language which is commonly characterized as linguistic turn in philosophy. It is evident from a cursory look at the development of philosophy that language becomes an independent subject of study. We are thus no longer surprised when we are offered philosophical theories in the form of linguistic proposals. Geilbert Ryle goes to the extent of saying that "philosophical arguments have always, if not entirely, consisted in attempts to thrash out 'what it means to say so and so'".[1] The concern for meaning and the correct characterization of the nature of meaning thus become the foremost concern of contemporary philosophy.

Philosophers' occupation with meaning is characterized by such general questions like: "what is meaning?", "how is meaning determined?", "how do expressions get their meaning?", etc. True, these are general questions but they cannot be answered in general terms. These questions cannot be answered independently of any perspective. They are semantic perspectives in the light of which meaning is characterized. This allows the possibility of alternative

---

[1] Rorty 1967: 85.

characterizations of meaning structure or semantic structure of natural language.

The two semantic perspectives that dominate the philosophers' discussion on meaning are: meaning atomism and meaning holism. As the name suggests, meaning atomism views meaning works atomistically. It is a view which suggests the meaning of a proposition is determined in isolation from other propositions. The reason behind claiming so is to support the correspondence theory of truth. This says that the meaning of a proposition expresses a state of affairs and if the state of affairs is found in the phenomenal world then the proposition will be treated as true and if it is not found in the phenomenal world then the proposition will be treated as false. This view is supported by Frege, Early Wittgenstein, logical positivists, Russell and many others. The holistic perspective on meaning says that meaning of a proposition is not determined in isolation. It determines in relation to other propositions of a given language. In this case, meaning is not an isolated phenomenon. It is a corporate or a global phenomenon. Hence, on account of second view, meaning works in a holistic way. This suggests that to understand the meaning of a proposition we need to understand a set of proposition of that language.

The major focus of this study is to contrast these two perspectives or models on meaning and to evaluate them with a view to arrive at a conception of meaning that will correctly reveal the semantics of natural language.

The first half of the thesis is devoted to the discussion of various theories of meaning developed in the atomistic perspective on meaning. Then, it explains the problems in atomistic theory of meaning, i.e. how atomistic theory of meaning fails to capture the meaning in most of the cases of our language.

On the basis of this discussion attempts have been made to show that atomistic theory of meaning has failed to account for the many-sided nature of meaning? On the basis of the failure of atomistic theory of meaning we explore the alternative theory, i.e.

meaning holism. Although meaning holism has diverse versions as global holism, content holism (psychological), moderate holism and molecular holism we give our arguments to support the view on moderate holism. To establish this we have considered the arguments of Quine, Davidson and Later Wittgenstein. All these philosophers though hold meaning holism differ in their respective standpoints while proposing their holistic conception of meaning. However, all of them agree on a common feature that the meaning of a proposition cannot be determined in isolation. Meaning can be decided in relation to a set of propositions in a particular paradigm of language.

In view of the stated objectives the inquiry to be undertaken in this study has the following structure conceived in terms of eight chapters. A brief description of each chapter is given below.

Chapter 1 is about the two conceptions of meaning. First conception, i.e. "meaning atomism", states that meaning of a sentence is determined in isolation from other sentences. This conception of meaning states that each sentence has some specific sense and is about the state of affairs of the world. The sentence will be meaningful if the state of affairs is found in the phenomenal world. So there is a tight-knit association between meaning of a proposition and its referred state of affairs. This explains that every proposition is either true or false. The proposition will be treated as true if the state of affairs maps the empirical world and it will be treated as false if the state of affairs does not map the empirical world. Hence, truth-value of a proposition is determined by its referred state of affairs. The important idea of this conception of meaning is that the truth-value of a proposition determines the meaning of a proposition. Logically speaking, if a proposition does not have truth-value it will be regarded as a meaningless proposition.

Second conception, i.e. "meaning holism", elucidates the nature of meaning as a form of holism. It disagrees with the fact that meaning of a proposition is determined in isolation from other sentences. The reason is, meaning is not an isolated phenomenon. It is an interconnected phenomenon. The meaning of a proposition is interconnected with other propositions. The meaning of a proposition is thus determined by a body of interconnecting propositions. Hence, meaning works holistically. The important issue involved in this conception of meaning is that between meaning and truth it is the determination of the meaning of a proposition and not the truth-value of a proposition that is emphasized.

Chapter 2 presents the atomistic theory of meaning in the light of Frege. Frege in his philosophical works repeatedly mentioned that meaning of a proposition is determined by the conditions of its applicability. In his paper "On Sense and Reference" he clearly points out that every proposition has a sense and it is of logical sort. Again, that sense is about the state of affairs of the world/facts of the world/objects of the world. A proposition will be treated as true if sense of that proposition agrees with the facts of the world. On the contrary, a proposition will be treated as false if sense of that proposition does not agree with the facts of the world. For him, sense of a proposition is same as thought of a proposition. Hence, every thought states something about the state of affairs of the world. On this account, he claims that meaning works atomistically. Further, he states that meaning of a proposition is determined in relation to its truth-value. So, the individual sentence plays a role for determining the meaning of a proposition. Hence, the individual sentence is self-sufficient for determining its meaning. Thus, his approach to meaning is considered as an atomistic one.

Early Wittgenstein's approach to meaning is dealt in Chapter 3. This chapter discusses how his approach to meaning supports the atomistic theory of meaning. His claim on atomistic theory of meaning is based on two views – picture theory of meaning and elementary proposition. In his view, every sentence depicts a picture. The picture is about the state of affairs of the world. The sentence will be judged as true if the picture maps the state of affairs of the world and it turns out to be false if the picture does not map the state of affairs of the world. Hence, truth-value of a sentence is determined by its picture, i.e. what the sentence states about. "Picture" of a sentence may be considered same as "sense" of a sentence or "essence" of a sentence.

According to him, all sentences can be reduced to atomic sentences which are also called elementary sentences. Atomic sentences are those which state the facts of the world. With the help of correspondence theory it is decided whether a sentence is true or false. Thus, truth or falsity of a sentence is decided on the availability of its corresponding state of affairs.

He states that the picture of a proposition is a logical one. By this he means the possible description of reality. The reality of a proposition is explained through two ways:

1. By explaining its sense.
2. By determining its truth conditions.

Sense reflects the picture in a proposition. A proposition will be true if the sense of that proposition agrees with reality and it will be false if it does not agree with the reality. Thus, "a proposition is a picture of reality" (*Tractatus* 4.12). This will enable us to bring out the truth condition of a proposition. He further states that every proposition can be judged as either true or false because all propositions endowed with "thought" and that are about the state of affairs of the world. Thus, he confirms that we cannot imagine a sentence without its truth condition. Hence, it is assumed that he is an atomist.

In the discussion of meaning, logical positivists make their significant contribution. They reject metaphysical statements as meaningless on the ground that they are not verifiable. Through their semantic critique of metaphysics they developed their own theory of meaning which says that meaning is a matter of empirical verification. Verifiability becomes a condition for a sentence to be meaningful. Hence, proposed as a criterion for meaningfulness. Subsequently, this criterion has been revised by logical positivists in a number of ways with a view to make their conception of meaning acceptable. Chapter 4 gives a detailed exposition of logical positivists' conception of meaning.

The main aim behind proposing verifiability theory of meaning is to reject metaphysical statement, on the one hand, and on the other hand, to establish a truth theory for determining the meaning of all statements.

Positivists claim that a proposition is factually significant when a person knows how to verify a proposition. To verify a proposition means to know the various observations under which the proposition will be true or false. In this respect, Waismann states that "a person who utters a proposition must know under what conditions the proposition is to be judged as true or false; if he is not able to specify that, he does not know what he has said" (Hanfling 1981a: 27). Further, logical positivists state that to understand a proposition means to know how things stand, i.e. what the proposition is stating about. Hence, a sentence is self-evident and self-sufficient for determining its meaning. In this regard, their view is considered as atomistic.

Why meaning atomism fails to capture the uniqueness of meaning is explained in Chapter 5. The question may be raised here is: What are the problems lie in atomistic theory of meaning for being qualified to be called a comprehensive theory of meaning? This chapter gives a few crucial arguments against atomistic theory of meaning. These arguments are: How picture theory of meaning is a valid theory? Do we verify all other propositions of a language when we understand a proposition? How to determine the sense of a proposition? Is it possible to refer to the actual state of affairs if we do not know the other states of affairs?

All these arguments together weaken the atomistic theory of meaning to justify its own standpoint. All these difficulties lead to the shifting of the alternative way for determining the meaning of a proposition, i.e. holistic conception of meaning. To determine the meaning of a proposition we require a body of propositions which is connected to the original proposition either directly or inferentially. Meaning in this way becomes a matter of interconnection between relevant propositions.

Chapter 6 discusses the theory of "meaning holism" in the light of Quine. Quine has borrowed the expression "meaning holism" from the physicist Duhem. Quine following Duhem arrives at an epistemological nature of meaning which says:

> The falsity of the observation categorical does not conclusively refute the hypothesis. What it refutes is the conjunction of sentences that was needed to imply the observation categorical. In order to retract that conjunction we do not have to retract the hypothesis in question; we could retract some other sentences of the conjunction instead. — Quine 1990: 13-14

This passage says that a hypothesis necessarily consists of a bunch of sentences. If the hypothesis goes wrong then one of the sentences of the bunch has to be modified or is to be replaced but this will not result into the replacement of the theory as a whole.

In a revised form Quine interprets the same concept in his own way: "No statement, taken in isolation from its fellows, admits confirmation at all. Our statements face the tribunal of sense experience only as a corporate body. Hence, it is not significant in general to speak of the confirmation of a single statement."[2]

To refute atomistic theory of meaning Quine has conceived of a strategy which consists of the following arguments. First, he rejects the distinction between analytic and synthetic statement claimed by logical positivists. Second, he brings out the fallacies of verificationists' theory of meaning. And, third, he formulates the indeterminacy of translation thesis to show the indeterminate nature of meaning. All these arguments have been discussed

[2] Wanger 1986: 1.

elaborately with a view to establish Quine's theory of meaning holism.

Chapter 7 is devoted to Davidson's approach to meaning holism. Here we have discussed how Davidson took the help from Tarski's T-Schema for establishing his own theory of meaning. Davidson's theory of meaning which he calls the theory of interpretation is based on three fundamental notions. These are, radical interpretation, belief system and the principle of charity. All these three notions together establish Davidson's theory of meaning holism. A detailed analysis of these three notions is given in this chapter.

On Davidson's account, a proposition cannot be self-sufficient for determining its meaning. The reason that he has given is that a proposition functions in a system of language. A language exhibits a network of propositions and beliefs being interconnected with each other. Thus, the determination of meaning of a proposition is not an isolated phenomenon. Rather it is a collaborative phenomenon. Hence, determination of meaning of a proposition needs other propositions situated in the same network. This is the way how meaning, as Davidson claims, works holistically.

Davidson, while explaining the radical interpretation, says that to interpret is to understand the fact that the speaker is expressing through his utterance. And to understand a fact implies understanding of some other related facts. In this sense, understanding assumes a network exhibiting the connection between propositions and beliefs. Hence, for him, holism is an authentic and genuine approach to meaning.

Later Wittgenstein's view on meaning holism is discussed in Chapter 8. The discussion highlights a few issues. First how use theory of meaning helps in determining the meaning of a proposition. Second, the role of language-game in determining the meaning of a proposition. And, third, the idea of family-resemblance for establishing the non-essentialistic conception of meaning. These are related issues which point out to Wittgenstein's inclination towards approaching meaning in holistic term.

The study concludes by arguing that meaning works holistically. The holistic approach to meaning as defined here is a moderate one. The idea of holism is defended here is neither global nor molecular. To say this is to accept the argument that for understanding a proposition we require a system of propositions within a particular paradigm of a language. This implies that we do not bring the whole language to understand a proposition. It is absurd to argue that to determine the meaning of a proposition we need to know the meanings of all possible propositions of that language. This view is supported by Michael Dummett. Dummett's arguments against global holism are discussed in this book with a view to arrive at a conclusion that a moderate holism may be viewed as the only acceptable form of meaning holism that can account for the semantics of natural language.

Satya Sundar Sethy

Contents

Acknowledgements

It is a pleasure duty to record my debts of gratitude.

I am very grateful to Prof. Amitabha Dasgupta, Dean of School of Humanities, University of Hyderabad, Telangana for his seamless inspiration, constant encouragement, valuable comments and suggestions while preparing this manuscript.

I am indebted to my parents for their ever-present love, constant support and encouragement. They are the source of inspiration for all my achievements and successes. What I am now is because of their grace, blessings and sacrifices.

It is a pleasure to acknowledge the constant inspiration and encouragement I received from my friend Anu to complete the book in time.

I am thankful to my colleagues of Department of Humanities and Social Sciences, Indian Institute of Technology Madras, Chennai for their encouragement and interest on the completion of this manuscript.

I am thankful to Prof. N.N. Chakraborty (Former Member Secretary of Indian Council of Philosophical Research, New Delhi), Prof. K. Srinivas (Department of Philosophy, Pondicherry University), Prof. Laxminarayan Lenka (Department of Philosophy, North-Eastern Hill University, Shillong) for their academic help and encouragement.

My sincere thanks to Centre for Continuing Eduction (CCE) of IIT Madras, Chennai for supporting me financially to write this manuscript.

I would also like to place on record my sincere appreciation for BTech students of IIT Madras to whom I taught "Meaning, Truth and Language" course in the last five years, whose feedback from time to time helped me develop certain arguments in this book.

IIT Madras, Chennai
February 2016

Satya Sundar Sethy

1

Two Conceptions of Meaning

LANGUAGE IS the medium of our communication. It consists of signs, words or combination of words. Meaning is central to communication because bare words and sentences are not communicable. So we need meaning in order to communicate our language. Meaning is the indispensable and inalienable aspect of language. There is no language without meaning. Thus, it cannot be dissociated from the language and in a wider sense, from the world and our living in it.

Meaning arises as the result of language-reality relationship, i.e. when language comes in contact with world. The word by itself has no meaning. It possesses meaning when it stands for something, for example, when we ask someone what the number "one" is, or, what the symbol *P*'1' means. In such occasions, we always refer to an object. But why is it so? Frege answers this question in an effulgent manner. He argues that the number "one" is not-nothing. Suppose if it were; wouldn't the word "one" be meaningless? It raises further an issue, i.e. if it is not-nothing, then what is it? It must be something, meaning thereby it must be about something. What remains are to say what kind of thing it is? Thus, the idea is that meaning is essentially a one–one relation between words and its corresponding objects. This solution gives rise to a further issue, i.e. how do we understand the meaning of words which do not correspond to objects? For example, words are like, "clarity", "colour", "honesty", "brevity", etc. do not correspond to any object. These words do not stand for any object yet we understand meaning of these words when we communicate in our language. Question arises how is it possible? Frege answers this by stating that "the meaning of an expression is not only a corresponding object but also a corresponding concept" (Parkinson 1988: 26). For example, consider a sentence "The number 4 is blue". Here, the number "4" as such does not correspond to any object. There is no object called "4". It is purely a thought – what Frege calls objective thought. Thus, it is a concept.

The notion of understanding is intrinsically related to the notion of meaning. Understanding an utterance involves understanding its meaning. According to Dummett, "the task of a theory of meaning is to give an account of how that language works" (Dummett 1993: 3). Thus for him, a theory of meaning is a theory of understanding. To understand a speaker's language means to understand the meaning of words or sentences uttered by that person. Therefore, meaning is an inseparable aspect of language.

There are two dominant conceptions of meaning: meaning atomism and meaning holism.

The structure of the two notions of meaning may be explained in the following way. In the framework of atomistic theory, the notion of meaning is viewed exclusively in relation to individual sentences. Thus understanding of meaning consists in understanding the meaning of individual sentences. The central feature of this conception (i.e. atomistic) of meaning is that it assumes an inseparable connection between meaning and truth. The meaning of a sentence is thus decided by its truth conditions. On the other hand, meaning is holistic because meaning is an interconnected phenomenon. It is not an isolated phenomenon. It is understood in relation with other phenomena. The entire language matters when we try to explain meaning of an individual sentence of a particular language. It is so, because sentences are interconnected with other sentences and thus involves a network of relationships.

Logically speaking, meaning atomism states that a linguistic expression *e* in a language *L* has its meaning by virtue of its symbol–world relationship which is independent of other expressions of *L*. In contrast to this, meaning holism expresses that a linguistic expression *e* in a language *L* has its meaning in virtue of its relations with other expressions *e* in *L*, i.e. in virtue of its role in *L*.

Atomistic Theory of Meaning

Meaning atomism roughly states that every representation either in linguistic or mental system is completely definable by itself. This theory identifies meaning with truth. To know the meaning of a sentence is to know the conditions under which the sentence is judged as true. In this connection Waismann says that "a person who utters a proposition must know under what conditions the proposition is to be called true or false; if he is not able to specify that, he does not know what he has said" (Hanfling 1981a: 27).

As it has been stated that in the atomistic theory of meaning, each sentence gets its meaning without relating to other sentences in a particular system which may be either linguistic or mental, it simply means that each sentence is self-sufficient and self-evident for establishing their truth. It is so, because each individual sentence expresses a fact and the fact states about the world. Here, when we claim that each sentence expresses the fact about the world, we really mean the reference of it. Thus, each sentence refers to the fact of the world. If the referent is found in the empirical world then the sentence is true, otherwise false.

A simple justification of the thesis can be given in the following argument:

A_1: The sentence "This is a pen" means that this is a pen.

A_2: "This is a pen" is true.

From these two propositions, it is concluded that

A_3: If a sentence *S* is true and *S* means *P*, then *P*.

The above constituents form the core of the "atomistic theory of meaning" and it dominates the semantic tradition since Frege.

According to Frege, a sentence must have "thought" but "thought" cannot be same as "meaning". He has given an example for proving it as follows:

i. The morning star is illuminated by sun.
ii. The evening star is illuminated by sun.

These two expressions have different meaning but their thought remains same. Thus he says:

> The thought, in itself immaterial clothes in the material garment of a sentence and thereby becomes comprehensible to us.
>
> — Frege 1956: 292

He points out that there must be something which is belonging to both expressions and which would remain invariant to the changes of "thought", is nothing but "truth". As a consequence, whenever we obtain the meaning of a sentence we need its truth-value. In his words, "by truth value of a sentence I understand the circumstance that it is true or false" (Geach and Black 1952: 63). Thus, to understand a proposition means to know what is the case if it is true.

"Meaning atomism" satisfies the following three requirements:

i. It must provide a theory describing the constituents of meaning, i.e. a specification of the representations that are semantic atoms.
ii. It should enable us to constitute a theory of definition that will specify how each non-atomistic component can be defined in terms of aggregate of atoms.
iii. It must specify the meanings of the atoms — a specification of what it is for atoms to have the particular meanings as they have.

The above description points out the linkage between the truth theory of meaning and the referential theory of meaning. To explain, referential theory states that meaning of a sentence is determined by its reference. Here, first of all, we are indicating the fact of the actual world and then claiming the sentence as true which is about that fact. Thus, it is expressed that in atomistic theory a proposition is true or false depends on its corresponding facts. The relation between a proposition and its truth-value is not like a relation between a table and its shape, but like between the sense of a definite description and the actual object for which it stands.

There are three primal issues revolving around the truth conditional approach to meaning. These are:

1. What is it for a word or expression to be meaningful?
2. What is it for a word or expression to mean what it does?
3. How does the meaning of a complex expression depend upon their parts?

Apart from all these issues there are some other issues also involved when we discuss meaning in relation to its truth conditional approach. These are:

i. What is the nature of meaning and truth?
ii. What are the criteria for determining the meaning and truth-value of a proposition?
iii. Why do we treat meaning and truth together?
iv. Can "truth" be treated independently of "meaning"?

"Truth" in the traditional philosophy deals with individual sentences. It states that "a true proposition is one which says that the state of affairs is so and so, and the state of affairs indeed is so and so" (Sen 1991: 6). This phrase states that truth of a proposition corresponds to a fact or a state of affairs where states of affairs are found in the empirical world in the form of object language. In this connection, we may have a passing reference to Davidson who defines truth theory in the light of object language.

Davidson has borrowed a schema or a framework called "Convention-T" from Tarski in order to define the truth characterization in meaning theory. By a "truth- characterization" of a sentence he means, how the predicate determines the truth of a sentence. His "Convention-T" explains how to construct a truth theory in formalized or ideal language. There are two basic principles required for satisfying "Convention-T". These are:

A theory of truth for a language L must be such that

i. For each sentence *S* of *L* a *T*-sentence should be provable.

ii. Each such provable *T*-sentence should be true.

Whatever language we express, it is in the form of object language but whatever we express on object language it entails to meta-language. Meta-language seeks to explain how object language functions in the corpus of that language of a particular system. As a result, it will help to establish the truth theory in the object language. Meta-language must meet the following requirements.

1. It must allow for all expressions of the object language to be explicable in it.
2. It must contain semantic concepts in relation to the object language that cannot be formulated in the object language.[1]

Tarski's explanation of truth theory is about the object language, where he states that how meta-language helps to explain the truth theory in the object language. A discussion on this problem will thus show how atomistic theory of meaning functions through the framework of truth conditional approach to meaning as constructed by Tarski.

Tarski and 'Convention-T'

Tarski's "T-Schema" is:

(*T*) *X* is true if and only if *P*.

It expresses the equivalence relation between *X* and *P*. Here *X* is the name of the sentence of the object language and *P* is the sentence of the object language. So *P* is the actual sentence and *X* expresses about *P*. For example, "'snow is white' is true if and only

[1] Ladislav 1996.

if snow is white in the empirical world". Here, we are deriving *X* from *P*, where *X* is the meta-language. This theory is known as "redundance theory" or "cancellatory theory" because we are going from "quotation" to "disquotation", in a way, we are going from language to the world.

In this schema, he focuses on the semantic concept of truth, which says that "to know the semantic concept of truth for a language is to know what it is for a sentence" (Davidson 1984: 24). Analysing the "*T*-Schema", he viewed that in order to understand the meaning of a sentence we require the features as, the theory must be finitely specifiable so that a finite speaker can grasp it. As a result, we can understand how a finite speaker could speak the language and what it is about.

Tarski in his paper "The Concept of Truth in Formalized Language" explains how we arrive a satisfactory definition of truth where individual sentence alone can be treated as either true or false. According to Davidson,

> A satisfactory theory of meaning must give an account of how the meaning of sentences depend on the meaning of words.
>
> – 1984a: 17

Unless such an account could be supplied for a particular language,

> it is argued that there would be no explaining fact that we can learn the language; no explaining fact that on mastering a finite vocabulary and a finitely stated set of rules, we are prepared to produce and to understand any of a potential infinitude of sentences. . . . I want to ask what it is for a theory to give an account of the kind adumbrated. — Ibid.

Tarski defines "truth" as, "*X* is a true sentence if and only if *X* is a sentence and every (infinite) sequence of objects satisfies *X*"[2] (Tarski 1956: 195). We accept this definition because it is "formally

[2] It is not strictly a definition. But the idea generated from Tarski might be projected in the form of a definition.

correct". In order to make it "material adequate", it needs to satisfy the condition "Convention-T" or "*T*-Schema". That is, "*X* is a true sentence if and only if *P*". On his view, two sentences have the same truth-value when they are materially equivalent. It is just like we know two lines have the same direction when they are parallel.

Further, he makes his point clear by stating that we need three features to determine truth-value of a sentence. These are:

i. To find out what the sentence says,
ii. Does it express a fact?, and finally,
iii. whether the fact is about the world?

Unless these three questions are answered, a sentence will remain irrelevant and incoherent for us.

There are sentences which vary from place to place, speaker to speaker, and time to time. In order to determine the truth-value of these sorts of sentence we need to accept Davidson's suggestion of how to relate sentences in accordance with speaker, time, and place.

Indexical Sentences

Davidson in his paper "Truth and Meaning" expresses that how indexical sentences are important for determining the truth-value of individual sentences. The analysis may be given in an exemplar form. In rainy season, leaves of the trees are green whereas, these leaves turn into yellow or red in summer season. If it is so, then how could we establish the truth of the proposition, "The leaves of the trees are green"? Another example, "I am tired". This sentence varies from person to person, place to place and time to time. A question arises, how could we establish its truth-value? In order to resolve these sorts of problem, Davidson has taken the help of "indexical sentence" which states that "truth" is a relation among a sentence, a person and a particular time. For example, "'I am tired' is true as spoken by *P* at *T* if and only if *P* is tired at *T*". Thus for him, truth must be empirical, which means something open for testing or verification.

Since all propositions have meaning and meaning helps to determine the truth-value of the propositions, it implies each proposition presupposes a "thought". This is so because thoughts are intrinsically related to the meaning of the propositions. In this regard, Frege states that all propositions are endowed with thought and they state about the world.

Frege's concern on truth-conditional approach to meaning is found in his work on *On Sense and Reference.* He defines meaning in terms of thought. For him, meaning of a sentence is same as a thought expressed in a sentence. Linguistic expressions are in the form of words or combination of words expressing the sense of thought. To know the sense of a proposition means to know the conditions of applicability of the world. More precisely, to know the sense of a word means to know what the word means and how it is to be applied. Thus, every proposition can be judged as either true or false because each proposition is endowed with "thought". He explains:

> The thought, in itself immaterial clothes in the material garment of a sentence and thereby becomes comprehensible to us.
>
> — Frege 1956: 292

Further he states that "by truth-value of a sentence I mean the circumstances that it is true or false" (Frege 1952: 63). Therefore, to understand a proposition for Frege is to know what is the case if it is true.

Since all propositions have thought and, therefore, can be judged as either true or false, Wittgenstein states that there must be something on thought that is invariant from speaker to speaker on a particular expression. Hence, it is viewed that "sense" is the logical content of a proposition and it lies in the possible descriptions of reality. The reality of a proposition is explained in terms of the following methods:

i. By explaining sense.

ii. By explaining truth conditions.

Sense reflects the picture in a proposition. The picture will be true if its sense agrees with reality, otherwise false. Thus, "a proposition is a picture of reality" (*Tractatus* 4.12). By the help of "explication" we can bring out truth condition of a proposition. He states that every proposition can be judged either true or false because all propositions are endowed with "thought" and expressing about objects of the world. Thus, he conceives that we cannot imagine a sentence without its truth conditions.

In this respect, logical positivists such as Carnap, Schlick, A.J. Ayer, Waismann, Moore and a few more are emphatically expressed that meaning of an expression or a proposition is associated with the cognitive use of language which implies whether a sentence is true or false. This criterion of meaningfulness is associated with the criterion of verifiability. The verifiability doctrine determines the truth of an actual fact and provides the necessary conditions for inquiring its truth. In this regard, Schlick points out that a person knows the meaning of a proposition if he is able to indicate the suitable circumstances under which it would be true and distinguishes from the circumstances under which it would be false. A point that is asserted here, if we know the meaning of a sentence *S*, then we know how to determine its truth-value. But if we are unable to determine the truth-values of *S*, this shows that we have not understood the sentence completely, i.e. we do not know the meaning of it. Thus, knowing the truth condition implies knowing the meaning and knowing the meaning implies knowing the truth condition. In this regard, "meaning" and "truth" are having the tight-knit association and it satisfies the atomistic theory, i.e. truth conditional approach to meaning.

Atomistic theory of meaning is insufficient to capture the complexity of meaning because this theory seeks to explain meaning only in relation to individual sentences. Individual sentences won't confirm our experience exclusively or completely on a particular object. In this regard, Quine states that a sentence could confirm our experiences only when it relates with other sentences within a particular paradigm. Thus, it works holistically.

Meaning Holism

Meaning is not an isolated phenomenon. It is an interconnected phenomenon. It cannot be separated from language. The whole of language matters when we try to explain meaning. Thus, language and meaning works together. They work holistically. We understand meaning of an expression only in relation to other expressions or concepts. Meaning of a concept is thus essentially connected to other concepts. This results into what is known as meaning holism, i.e. meaning is holistic in character.

Roughly speaking, in meaning holism, each representation in linguistic or mental system semantically depends on other representations of that system. In this context, it is warranted to discuss what exactly "meaning holism" is.

Meaning holism as a thesis has three constituents:

1. First of all, it is a theory.
2. A theory about interrelatedness of meaning of propositions.
3. Interrelatedness of meaning of propositions is conceived in a representational system which acts as a constituent to the theory.

Assume a system *S* and a representation *R*. Every representation of meaning in *S* virtually depends on the meaning of every other representations of *S*.[3] This holds the meaning holism of *S*. To clarify further, a system will be holistic if and only if properties of the part of a whole should be found within the whole.

In the holistic system, the representation *R* contains some other representations those are inferentially related to *R* is known as "inferential role semantics" (hence after, IRS).[4] For example, in order to understand the word "pen" we need to understand some other concepts, such as "writing", "white", "colour", and "ink". This is obvious because all these words are interlinked with each

[3] Lormand 1996.

[4] Ibid.

other in order to discern the particular concept "pen". Thus, to understand the meaning of a word it presupposes understanding of some other words in relation to that word. In this way, our understanding of a word is interlinked with some other words, as sentences are interlinked with other sentences. A question arises, is it possible for everyone to presuppose the same sort of words for understanding the concept "pen"? Holists state that these sorts of inference depend upon the speakers who are engaged in establishing the semantic linkages between words. To uphold this procedure holists relied upon the two following sources:

i. Speaker's general intelligence.

ii. Available information.

It is stated that "sense" of a word is based on the notion of primitive epistemic property. A property is one which is characterized by the relation of presupposition. Presupposition is a relation between two concepts where one presupposes the other for its understanding.[5] For example, in order to understand the term "room" we need to understand the terms like "brick", "sand", "iron" and "people". It is so, because these terms are interlinked in this way; "we need the materials as iron, brick and sands for constructing a building", "a building consists of few rooms", "each room is surrounded by four walls" and "the wall of a room is made by people". Therefore, understanding the term "room" presupposes that we have understood the term "people" already or, in other words, we had an idea of the term "people" before understanding the term "room". Thus, it is viewed that it is a set of epistemic property associated with these words that we need to know in order to find out "the walls of a room is made by people". A "word" is not just mere a word. It is a concept. It may be presented in the form of a sentence. Thus, sentences similar to words function holistically. Hence, holism becomes the part of a linguistic behaviour.

[5] This idea has been suggested by Carlo Penco 2002.

In a holistic system, we find that there is a semantic dependence between each representation (say, R_1, R_2, R_3, etc.) occurring in a particular system. If it is so, then a question erupts "what sort of semantic dependence do we find among the representations of a holistic system?" The answer is an "ontological dependence" which binds every representation together in a holistic system.

There are two sorts of ontological dependence. These are:

1. Rigid ontological dependence.
2. Generic ontological dependence.

These two principles are elucidated with the help of an example, as follows:

> An ontological dependence is "rigid" if and only if an individual *X* cannot exist unless an individual *Y* exists. Hence, if *X* exists in a possible world then *Y* must exist in that world. Contrast to this, ontological dependence is "generic" if and only if an individual *M* cannot exist unless there are some other individuals characterized as *M* kind must exist along with it. Thus, if *M* exists in a possible world then some other individuals similar to *M* must exit in that world. For example, suppose a few members of a social community may die and new members are born in that community, the remaining members of the community will be regarded as the same thinking being and the community will remain the same as community.[6]

In a holistic view, it is not only necessary that if there is an *X*, there must be some other individual *Y* but also if there is a *Y*, there must be some other individual *X* exists too. In this way the parts of a holistic system are dependent on each other. Thus, we need both sorts of dependence in a holistic theory.

"Meaning holism" has two phases,[7] such as:

---

[6] The distinction between two sorts of dependence is suggested by Simons 1987. In this connection, please see also Esfeld 1998.

[7] Lormanad 1996.

1. All-or-none
2. At-least-some.

To explain:

Consider a system *S* and a representation *R*. The holistic system states that a representation *R* which is containing some other representations are inferentially related to *R*. Judging the first phase "all-or-none", it is stated that there is no clear-cut distinction found between:

1. inferential representation of *R*, and
2. the irrelevant representation of *R*.

Thus, the representation *R* either semantically depends on all other representations of the system *S* completely or none of them. This distinction states that either we have to accept "extreme holism" or "extreme localism".[8] On the other hand, the phase "at-least-some" claims that the representation *R* of the system *S* cannot be wholly or completely independent of other representations of the system *S*. This amounts to accepting holism and rejecting atomism.

In "meaning holism" we find two primary issues. These are:

1. What sort of dependence do we find among meanings of a holistic theory?
2. What sort of meaning that constitutes when we say that every representation is dependent on each other in a holistic system?

Considering the first and foremost question it is explained that there are two sorts of dependence:

---

[8] The phrase "extreme holism" is defined as; each sentence depends on the meaning of other sentences for acquiring its meaning. On the other hand, "extreme localism" emphasizes on the individual sentence and explains how individual sentences are self-sufficient for acquiring its meaning. This shows that individual sentences do not need any further sentences to get their meaning.

i. Influential dependence.

ii. Differential dependence.

X influentially depends on *Y*. Their dependence is very minute. Logically speaking, if *Y* were to differ, *X* would differ, but not necessarily. So it will not satisfy the holistic nature of meaning. On the other hand, the "differential dependence" principle claims that if *Y* were to differ, *X* would differ. For example, in English language, the term "milk" and "white" are differentially dependent on each other on the basis of their meaning. The reason is: if somehow the term "milk" changes its meaning, then "white" has to change its status (meaning). Thus, the second one is stronger than the first one. As a result, meaning holism supports the "differential dependence" rather than "influential dependence".

Regarding the second issue, holists claim that "multiple meaning" is one of the solutions for establishing meaning holism.[9]

Multiple Meaning

Multiple meaning is the result of the potential causal/inferential links in which a given concept might participate. These multiple meanings are divided into some classes and each class forms one "unit". For example, consider the term "bird":

B_1: first unit is associated with bird as "feathered flying animal".

B_2: second unit is "thing called a bird by mommy".

B_3: third unit is "thing that is in similar to $B_1, B_2, \ldots B_n$".[10]

Multiple meanings claim that each unit associates with a representation constituting one of its meanings. Each representation may have as many meanings as it has units. Thus, in order to get the meaning of a word we are supposed to think of the meaning of a concept as the collection of all of its individual meanings.

Further, it is stated that two representations may have different

---

[9] Lormanad 1996.

[10] Ibid.

sorts of units, still they share meaning with each other. This is possible if the meaning of a particular unit of a representation overlaps with the meaning of the unit of other representation even though there may be changes found in the rest of the units. Thus, though a unit changes for a representation, the meaning of the term remains same as it was before. In other words, the meaning of a representation will be the same as it was earlier. This simply proves the stability of meaning in a representational system, which is the basic requirement for establishing the holistic theory.

True, overlapping of units accounts for meaning stability which will ultimately establish meaning holism. But it can be shown that even though there may be meaning stability, it cannot establish meaning holism satisfactorily. We explain this in the following way. Meaning stability states that meaning of each representation depends on the meaning of other representations for acquiring its meaning. Since each representation is depending on every other representation, changing the meaning of one representation affects the meaning of other representations. The change of meaning of a representation means our belief relating to that representation changes. Believing a representation we mean, an attitude of a speaker who intends to accept any sentence without knowing the truth-value of the sentence.[11] It is an attitude may be applicable to all sentences. Thus, the problem of representational system is the problem of our "belief system". Here, a question arises, i.e. if our belief changes for a concept then the meaning of a concept will also change. But, then, how does it sustain the "meaning stability" in a representational system? In order to make it more clear let us give an example. Tom acquires a new belief about the term "feathered" for having a concept on the term "bird". This belief changes the unit of the meaning of the term "bird", i.e. "feathered flying animal". Hence, the concept "bird" changes.

---

[11] I used the term "belief" following Davidson's analysis of belief as suggested in his paper "Radical Interpretation".

In order to resolve this problem holists have given an example as follows. Tom and Tic are living in different places having different cognitions relating to the term "bird". For Tom, the mental representation of "bird" is associated with some units:

1. Feathered flying animal, and
2. things called "bird" by mummy.

Similar to above sentences, there may be many other ways of describing the meaning of the term "bird".

In other side of Tic she is blind from her childhood. She has a mental representation "bird" which is associated with one unit. That is "thing called a bird by mummy". Here we find that these two persons are capable of having agreement and disagreement precisely because they share one common unit with each other, i.e. "things called bird by mummy". As a result, both of them understand the term "bird". It is possible because the overlapping unit holds the "meaning stability" which is the basis for establishing meaning holism.

In this connection, Hilary Putnam states that it might be the case where two persons may learn the same expression through different trainings, therefore through different inferences, both of them can understand what the word means and what it stands for. For example, John offering a fruit named "strawberry" to Jack. Here John is a boy who is living in a remote village. For him:

i. Strawberry is a fruit.
ii. It is found in countryside.
iii. Used to pick strawberries in fields after sunrise.
iv. It is red in colour.
v. It is sweet in taste.
vi. To be taken as free of cost.
vii. It is edible.

Whereas Jack as a city boy understands the term "strawberry" as:

a. Strawberry is a fruit.
b. It is found in super market.
c. It is green in colour.
d. It is sweet in taste
e. It is very expensive.

Though John and Jack have understood the term "strawberry" differently, yet they share some common meaning with each other. As a result, if one utters "have strawberries!" the other person understands it. Further, question arises, if two persons differ completely about their expressions of a particular object then how communication will take place between them. Holists resolve this problem by giving a suitable example as follows:[12]

Strawberry for John	*Strawberry for Jack*
Red fruit	Green fruit
Edible and sweet	Not edible; ornamental
To be picked up from fields	It is available only in shops
It is available free of cost	It is available only on payment

In this case, no property is shared between two speakers, but the property of attaching a name "strawberry" to an object such as a fruit or a vegetable is common for both of them. The communication will be possible between John and Jack, if John will succeed in making Jack understand that strawberry is present and is to be eaten, or at least "strawberry" is a word referring to what he has in his hand.

However, the stability of meaning of a concept is found in some senses but not in all senses. For example, considering a concept "bird", Tom erroneously believes that birds sometimes

[12] Penco 2002.

make croaking sounds and Tic is afraid of them, while Tic correctly believes that "frog" sometimes makes croaking sounds. In this case "Tom" is saying something more about the concept "bird" whereas, Tic is saying more about a "frog" than a "bird". Thus, it is stated that "meaning stability" is possible due to the stability of the "units", which constitute the various meanings of a representation.

The holistic theory provides all the psychologically relevant meanings that referential theories completely omit. Thus psychologically relevant meanings are more fine-grained than referents (objects). It is because of psychology, which is supposed to require taxonomy (classification) of mental representations. It is responsible for psychological generalization. When meaning holism is applied to mental content, the content of a concept depends upon its relation to most other concepts in an internal system of the representation. Thus, it is stated that meaning of either a term or a sentence cannot be understood individually or independently without relating to other terms and sentences. Therefore, meaning works holistically.

2

Frege and Atomistic Theory of Meaning

MEANING IS an inalienable property of language and it is understood in different ways. Some of the well-known ways by which it is understood are: as the property of sentences, as the use, as the representation in the sense of a picture of a sentence and also as the relation to truth condition. Traditionally, meaning atomism or the atomistic perspective on meaning is a very important conception of meaning which identifies meaning with reference. In this chapter we will discuss the issues of meaning as advocated by Frege. His atomistic theory of meaning is constructed through his truth-conditional approach to meaning. Thus the idea of meaning defined in terms of truth conditions has become the predominant tradition in semantics due to Frege.

We have stated in the first chapter that meaning atomism states that every representation either in a linguistic or in a mental system is completely definable by itself. To say that meaning is completely definable is to lay emphasis on the individual sentences because it is the individual sentence that matters in our concern for meaning. The truth-conditional approach to meaning has been developed from the same semantic presupposition, i.e. the individual sentence as the basic unit of language. To know the meaning of a sentence is to know the conditions under which the sentence is true. Thus understanding of meaning consists in understanding the meaning of individual sentences. The central feature of this conception of meaning (meaning atomism) is that it assumes an inseparable connection between meaning and truth. Thus, meaning of a sentence is so conceived that it is decided by its truth condition. The truth conditional approach to meaning in this sense expresses meaning atomism.

In Frege the idea of atomistic theory of meaning and its analysis are primarily developed in his paper "On Sense and Reference". He states that in order to have a meaningful sentence it should fulfil the criterion of "sense". Though the term "meaning" is not same as the term "sense" as understood by Frege, yet sense may be understood broadly under the larger domain of meaning.

Frege's Notion of Sense and Reference

Frege, in his paper "On Sense and Reference" clearly points out that "sense" is the first and foremost criterion for having a meaningful sentence. Sense is the thought which is expressed in a sentence. So, it helps to get the reference of a proposition. Sense is always logically prior to reference. In order to refer to something we must understand the meaning of a word or a sentence that it stands for. Thus, sense is the medium through which we refer to something. For Frege, reference of a sentence is nothing but the truth-value of that sentence. A sentence possesses meaning implies that it can be judged as either true or false.[1] In this connection, we should keep in our mind that Frege is not interested in psychological issues concerning meaning. His primary interest lies with the issues concerning the empirical world.

Let us consider the sentence, "The grass is green". Since it is an atomic sentence it does not require any further sentence to establish its truth-value. It is so, because atomistic sentences are self-sufficient and self-evident for establishing their truth-value. The sentence, "The grass is green" is true because it corresponds to the object called grass whose colour is green. A question is raised here, "Can meaning be purely defined in truth-conditional terms?" In order to resolve this problem, Frege makes a distinction

---

[1] These two concepts, one is, reference of a sentence is same as truth-value of that sentence and another is, meaningful sentences can be judged as either true or false, are borrowed from Perry 1977.

between "sense" and "reference". The analysis of this distinction between sense and reference is based on the puzzle between identity statements.

The term "identity" is first of all a relation. It is a relation between things, and further, the minimum requirement of the relation is that at least it must be holding between the two. Suppose, *A* and *B* are two different expressions. The identity relation between *A* and *B* states that "*A* coincides with *B*" or "*A* is similar with *B*". Let us take an example.

i. $A = A$.

ii. $A = B$.

In the first case, we are not getting any new information, because it is just the repetition, whereas in the second case, we are getting some new information based on the cognitive value of the expressions.

Let us take a look at the famous example cited by Frege:

1. The morning star is same as morning star.
2. The morning star is same as evening star.

The first proposition states that "the morning star" is identical with "the morning star" and it is known by the principle of analyticity and synonimity. So, it is true by virtue of its definition. On the other hand, the second proposition gives us the information that "the morning star" is same as "the evening star". This identity is derived from the empirical discovery. This sentence is true by virtue of our experience. Both the above propositions are true. However it is noticed that these two propositions differ in their meaning but not with their reference, since they refer to the same object called "Venus". A question is raised here, i.e. if meanings of the two propositions differ then how can we claim that they are identical with each other. Frege answers that sentences possess meaning when their constituent parts are having a specific meaning and they correspond to the specific object. This analysis is found in his "compositionality theory of meaning". Further, he states that meaning of an expression is unchanged if we substitute one expression with other which has the same reference.

Frege has taken three arguments for explaining the identity relation. The identity relation holds between the:

a. Objects

b. Names

c. Signs of objects

Considering the third issue, he states that "signs" are not arbitrary. It has a definite sense. The difference between two signs can arise when their mode of presentation differs from each other. For example,[2]

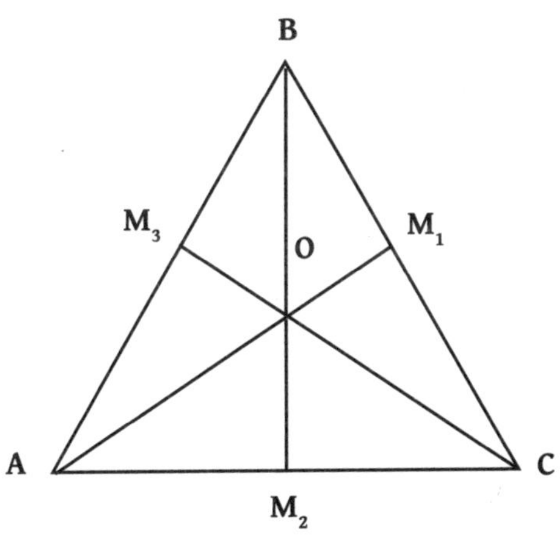

In this triangle, the point of the intersection between *A* and *B* is the referring expression and the expressions M_1 and M_2 designate the referent *O*. The point *O* is a referent which is an object. The point of the intersection between *B* and *C* designates *O*. Thus M_1, M_2 and M_3 are the referring expressions and they designate the object called *O*. So *O* is the referent.

[2] This graph has been taken from Munitz 1981: 112, for our own analysis.

Regarding the second issue Frege states that singular term or expression is called proper name. Let us consider two proper names "morning star" and "evening star". If we make the identity relation between these two proper names, we will find the following propositions.

i. Morning star is same as evening star.
ii. Morning star is same as morning star.
iii. Evening star is same as evening star.

The first proposition is a contingent truth because the identity relation between two proper names is known through empirical discovery whereas, second and third propositions are always true because of their logical necessity. They are true by virtue of their definitions. So we find two types of propositions, namely, analytic and synthetic. Here, we find three differences between two sorts of propositions.

1. The first proposition is a contingent truth whereas the second and third propositions are necessarily true.
2. The first proposition is an a posteriori truth whereas the other two propositions are true a priorily.
3. The first proposition is informative whereas the other two propositions are uninformative.

The above distinctions imply that someone can know "the evening star is the evening star" without knowing that the evening star is same as the morning star even though the evening star is same as the morning star. This is so because "evening star is the evening star" is just the repetition whereas "evening star is the morning star" is known through astronomical discovery.

Considering the first case (i.e. the identity relation between two objects), we find three different issues. These are as follows:

i. One and the same object may refer to two things. (For example, Venus is a planet referred to both morning star and evening star.)

ii. Two objects may refer to one thing as A. (For example, morning star and evening star are referred to one object called Venus.)

iii. Two objects may refer to two things — *A* and *B*, respectively.

For Frege, we get the sense of a sentence because of the functions of its constituent parts. In order to know the meaning of a sentence we need to know the meaning of its constituent parts and what they refer to. So every meaningful sentence must have a reference. Further, he states that expression without reference is not necessarily meaningless. It is so because there are cases where the propositions have meanings but do not refer to any object. For example, "Honesty is desirable". This proposition has sense, as a result, we understand what it expresses. But the constituent parts of this sentence do not refer to any object. There are no such objects called honest and desire found in this phenomenal world. So, this proposition has sense but not reference.

A question is raised here, how do we acquire the sense of a proposition? The answer is given by Frege. According to him, a proposition is constituted with some words and each word has a specific meaning. Words have meaning but they are not meaning themselves. When we classify words as meaningful and meaningless, we just describe the situations where they are acting as successful symbols and where they are not. By elaborating more he states that if I know the meaning of a word, then I have also known in what combinations it can occur and in what combinations it cannot. For example, if I know the meaning of the word "rain" then I can understand the following propositions:

i. It is raining.

ii. He was fond of preserving the rainwater.

In this way we can acquire the sense of the propositions.

But, there are some words, such as celestial city, craving, anxiety, honesty, punctuality that do not refer to anything. So how is it possible for us to get the meanings of those sentences (propositions) which are made of such words? Frege answers that the meaning of an expression not only corresponds to object, but also to concept.[3] For example, "Mr. *X* died in 1942". In this sentence, "Mr. *X*" does not have a referent. So in order to understand the meaning of this sentence we refer to the concept that "Mr. *X*" was a person who died in 1942 and is no more in this world. Here, we refer to the concept but not to the object. Thus we get the sense of this sentence. Further, if we examine some of the stanzas of a poem, we find that the poet due to his imaginations or speculations writes those. So the stanzas of the poem do not correspond to any object but correspond to the concept. Hence, we are able to get the sense of the stanzas of the poem, which may be represented in the form of assertive sentences. In this David Bell (1996: 589) points out that if we have a stock of concepts and if we bring them together with their logical necessity and applicability, we can produce a new concept. Hence, we can refer to that concept. For example, by combining the concepts "fox" and "female" we can have a new concept called "vixen", which can serve as a referent.

Frege states that to know the sense of a proposition means to know the conditions where it is to be applied. Hence, we know its applicability to the world. He used the philosophical terms "mode of presentation" and "mode of applicability" to explain this point. Sense of a proposition depends on its mode of presentation, whereas reference of a proposition relies on its mode of applicability. These two modes prone to state that to know the sense of a proposition means to know how to express the proposition, and to know how to express the proposition means to know the conditions where it is to be applied. Thus we arrive at the sense of a given proposition.

Sense is logically prior to reference. It is the sense that leads us to towards reference. It is so because unless we know the sense of a proposition, we cannot know what it expresses. Thus, sense assists

---

[3] Parkinson 1988: 26.

us to identify the referent of an object or a concept. A pertinent question is raised here, how does the sense of a sentence determine the reference?

Sense Determination and Reference

Sense is a passage through which we reach reference. To quote Dummett in this context:

> The sense of an expression is what we know when we understand it, and what we know when we understand it is something like an ideal procedure for determining its reference —Perry 1977: 475

Frege's notion of "sense" is applied to all-including "proper names". Now the question before us is, "Do proper names have sense?" Frege's reply to this question is that all proper names have a particular "sense", but they differ only in "opinions". Though opinions differ from person to person on a particular object, the sense is invariant to all. For example, in order to explain a proper name "Aristotle" there can be different descriptions, such as "the pupil of Plato", "the teacher of Alexander the great", "the author of *Nicomachean Ethics*", yet the sense of the term "Aristotle" remains same for all those who are using different descriptions. It is so because all of them understand the proper name "Aristotle" and do communicate in the language.

Frege's notion of sense is analysed in the following passage which he had written to his friend Philip Jourdain in 1914:

> Suppose an explorer is travelling in an unexplained country and sees a high snow-capped mountain on the northern horizon. By making inquires among the natives he learns that its name is "Afla". By detecting it from different parts he determines its position as exactly as possible, enters it in a map, and writes in his diary: "Afla" is at least 5,000 m. high. Another explorer sees a snow-capped mountain on the southern horizon and learns that it is called Ateb. He enters it on his map under that name. So, both of them enter the mountain on their respective maps under different names. Later comparison shows that both explorers

> saw the same mountain. Here, the geographical knowledge of that particular mountain which is presented in different names is same. Thus, the thought expressed in the proposition "Ateb is Afla" would have to coincide with the proposition "Ateb is Ateb" and "Afla is Afla". Before exploring "Ateb is same as Afla", it is certainly marked that "Ateb is Afla" is not the same thing as the content of proposition "Ateb is Ateb". If we correspond to the name "Ateb" as part of our thought, it refers to one object called snow-capped mountain. In the similar fashion, if we refer to the name "Afla", it corresponds to the same object as snow-capped mountain. Thus it is resulted that, the reference for both the names, Afla and Ateb is same whereas their sense differs from each other.[4] — Frege 1997: 320-21

From the above passage it follows that though these two expressions "Ateb is Ateb" and "Ateb is Afla" have different sense, both of them refer to one and the same object.

Frege states that "sense" of an expression is not associated with our psychology because psychology is a mental phenomenon which varies from speaker to speaker and speaker to hearer. But it is something which is objective, eternal and exists timelessly. For example, it is true that "water flows down" and would have been true even if there had been no being on the earth. Thus what is true is a thought, and a thought is the sense of a proposition.

Further, Frege states that sense is intrinsically, inherently and logically connected to a proposition. By giving an analogy he states that sense is the immaterial garment of material cloth of a proposition.[5] Thus sense is objective, eternal and at the same time communicable. He expresses that the sense of a proposition is same as the thought of a proposition.[6] Since every sentence is embedded with sense, all sentences must have thoughts. As a result,

---

[4] This passage presented in a precise form is borrowed from Frege 1997. See Noonam 2001: 169-70.

[5] The Idea is expressed in Frege 1977: 1-30.

[6] See Dummett 1991a.

all sentences can be judged as either true or false. In other words, all sentences can have the truth-value.

There are cases where different sentences of ordinary language have same truth-value but differ in their meanings. For example,

i. The author of *Nicomachean Ethics*

ii. The pupil of Plato.

These two expressions have different meanings but they refer to one and the same individual "Aristotle". So these two expressions have the same referent. Therefore, they have the same truth-value. It is so because for Frege reference of a sentence is same as truth-value of that sentence. Further, he suggests that two different sentences have same truth-value if they refer to one and the same object.

As it has been stated earlier that every sentence has a sense and from sense we can go to the reference. It implies that we refer to the object what the sentence is stating about. In this context Dummett points out that sense is key to our understanding of sentences and helps to determine truth-value of sentences. Further, he adds that what we know when we understand a proposition is something like an ideal procedure for determining its reference. There are two sorts of reference such are:

i. Word-reference.

ii. Sentence-reference.

In case of word-reference, the domain or the range of object is fixed but in case of sentences, they do not only refer to the thoughts of the expressions but also can be judged as either true or false. For Dummett, every thought can be assessable if it is found in the empirical world. In this sense, thoughts and language are interlinked with each other. As Bell puts it, "a thought of mine can be put into a form of words which will be understood by someone else to whom the thought is entirely new" (Bell 1996: 585). In this connection, Frege states:

> it is astonishing what language can do. With a few syllables it can express an incalculable number of thoughts, so that even if a thought has been grasped by an inhabitant of the earth for the very first time, a form of words can be found in which it will be understood by someone else to whom it is entirely new. This would not be possible, if we could not distinguish parts of the thought corresponding to the parts of a sentence, so that the structure of the sentence can serve as a model of the structure of the thoughts. — Frege 1984: 390

Further, David Bell while characterizing thought says that it is "communicable, expressible, inter-subjective, and above all, capable of being objectively true or false" (Bell 1996: 586). In this regard, Frege holds:

> A thought of which we are conscious is connected in our mind with some sentence or other is necessary for us humans. But that does not lie in the nature of the thoughts, but in our own nature. There is no contradiction in supposing there to exist beings that can grasp the same thought as we do without needing to clad it in a [linguistic] form. . . . But still, for us human beings there is this necessity. — Frege 1979: 269

On the above account, it is conceived that thoughts are logically embedded with the propositions. So every proposition is endowed with thought. As a result, every proposition can be judged as either true or false. More to say, thoughts are invariant and logically coherent with the propositions. Thoughts are objective, eternal, shareable and transmitted from generation to generation. Thus, thoughts do not belong to any psychological activity where mental phenomenon is one of the features. Frege made it clear by stating that thoughts are not acts of thinking because an act of thinking is a psychological process whereas thoughts are not. The apprehension of thought is called thinking. In thinking we do not produce thoughts but simply apprehend them. When we are thinking about thoughts, we may refer to them without expressing them. For example, I am thinking, "the weakest additional premise that would make the argument valid".[7] Here we are referring to that proposition which is represented in the form of a premise in the argument without expressing that proposition.

Thought of a proposition is found in the content of that proposition. Hence, content of a proposition can be shared with thought of that proposition. In this connection, David Bell states that "if one sentence involves a concept that another sentence does not involve, the two sentences cannot express the same thought nor have the same content" (Bell 1996: 588). Concerning this view, Frege affirms that thought is invariantly and logically related with propositions. As a result, we are able to determine the truth-value of propositions. A question is raised here: "Are thoughts same as ideas?" In order to resolve this problem Frege makes a distinction between "thought" and "idea". On his view, ideas are subjective whereas thoughts are objective and eternal. The reasons are as follows:

i. Ideas cannot be seen, touched, smelled and tasted. It is the impression of an observer which stored in his/her mind. More precisely, ideas cannot be presented to our sense-organs. For example, I saw a beautiful landscape. I have a visual impression on that landscape. I have it but I don't see it.

ii. An idea, which someone has, belongs to the content of his or her consciousness. The contents might be in the form of sensations, feelings, moods, inclinations, wishes, etc. For example, suppose a person is very much fond of apple. Once he had gone to a fruit vendor to purchase apple. The fruit vendor arrange different varieties of fruits including apple in his rickshaw. The person who had gone to purchase apple may see different fruits arranged systematically in vendor's rickshaw, but his content of consciousness (alertness) is on apple. So the idea of apple exists for him. Thus, it is stated that

---

[7] This example is taken from Dummett 1991a: 309.

without a bearer an idea cannot exist. In a similar fashion, an experience is not possible without an experiencer.

iii. Things of the outer world are independent of its bearer. However, ideas need a bearer. Ideas are subjective. Since ideas are subjective, they differ from individual to individual. A particular object is recognized by some people. Their ideas on that particular object may differ from person to person because their approaches may differ to that object. For example, some people see an animal named "Bucephalus" as a horse. Their ideas of that horse may differ, as the zoologist's idea of that animal "Bucephalus" may differ from the idea of a poet, and the idea of a poet may differ from the idea of a horse rider and so on. Hence, each idea needs a bearer. Without a bearer an idea cannot exist.

iv. Two individuals cannot have the same idea on a particular object because every idea needs only one bearer, and ideas are subjective. So, no two men have the same idea. For example, suppose I am having toothache and feel its pain. No other person can share my pain but someone may have sympathy for me. So here, my pain always belongs to me and his sympathy belongs to him. Hence, he does not have my pain and I do not have his sympathy. So, each idea has one and only one bearer. If it will be more than one, then ideas will be regarded as objective and universal, but it is not the case.

If ideas need a bearer then question arises, who is the bearer of my idea as "myself"? The answer given by Frege is, "I am" the idea of "myself". Here, I have an idea of myself but I am not identical with this idea.[8] So the content of my consciousness is "my idea" which could be sharply distinguished from what is an object of my thought on "myself". It will be clear if we explain this by the help of an analogy. In a strict and logical sense, I can see others as

[8] Frege 1977: 22.

in the form of objects, but I cannot see myself as an object. Frege asserts that I may see myself by gathering the impressions which I could get from the mirror. Thus, ideas need a bearer and without bearer ideas have no existence. It is just like if there is no ruler, there are no subjects.

On Frege's account, ideas are the power of thought and immediate objects of apperception. At the same time ideas correspond to the apprehension of thought. In thinking we do not produce thoughts but we apprehend them. When there is an idea, it is an idea of someone. It belongs to someone and is known to someone. On the contrary, a thought is transmitted from one generation to another. Thus, ideas are subjective and personal whereas thoughts are objective and eternal. In this regard, Frege argues that senses of expressions are unlike ideas on the ground that a particular sense, which an individual attaches to his or her words, can be grasped by others. But in the case of ideas it is not possible. Thus, he says that two speakers attach the same sense to their respective expressions only if they know that their expressions have the same referent.[9]

According to Frege,

> By a thought I understand not the subjective performance of thinking but its objective content which is capable of being the common property of several thinkers. — Frege 1952: 62

Further he states:

> Every sentence has a thought because the thought is in itself immaterial clothes found in the material garment of a sentence and thereby becomes comprehensible to us. — Frege 1956: 292

Thus every sentence expresses a thought. Since every statement expresses thought, it states about the facts of the world. So there

[9] Here, the term "sense" is used logically by replacing the term "thought". The term "sense" and "thought" are interchangeable, because both are synonymously used in Fregean context.

is a correspondence between the sense of a proposition and the facts of the world. Hence, all propositions can be judged as either true or false. To put it in Frege's words, "by truth-value of a sentence I mean the circumstances that it is true or false" (Frege 1952: 63). Thus, to understand a proposition means to know what is the case if it is true.

Frege holds that different propositions may express the same thought. In other words, a given thought can be adequately expressed by a number of structurally dissimilar sentences, yet their truth-value will remain same. For example,

i. The drawer is empty.

ii. There is nothing in the drawer.

iii. The number of things in the drawer is zero.

These three sentences differ in their structure. Some are quantified and others are not, some are expressed in negative terms and others are not, some are having *n*-ary predicate and some are not, yet all those sentences express one and the same thought. It is so because anyone who has grasped the thought of the above three propositions must be able to recognize one as true only if (s)he recognizes the others as true. This is possible because the content of the propositions are the same. A few examples of this similar type are:

a. (i) For every X, $T(x) \Leftrightarrow M(x)$.

(ii) The value range of T = the value range of M.

b. (i) Line *X* is parallel to line *Y*.

(ii) The direction of line *X* is the direction of line *Y*.

The content of a sentence exists independently of us but we can grasp them only by imposing propositional structure on them. According to Frege, contents are split into thoughts and truth-values. "Truth-value" itself has no structure, whereas every thought has a specific content. Therefore, it is structured as Dummett says (Dummett 1991: 305). Hence, it is widely accepted that the structure of a sentence serves as a model of the structure of a thought. In this connection, Russell asked Wittgenstein, if thoughts are well structured, can you elucidate the nature of thoughts and the elements that comprise them? It is cited as,

> Russell wrote to the author of the *Tractatus* asking for elucidation about the nature of thoughts and the elements that comprises them. Wittgenstein replied, I don't know what the constituents of a thought are, but I know that it must have such constituents which correspond to the words of language.
>
> — Wittgenstein 1974: 72

From this, it is presumed that each thought corresponds to the words of language.

Analysing further, Frege argues:

> If one sentence involves a concept that another sentence does not involve, the two sentences cannot express that same thought or have the same content. — Dummett 1991: 295

In his words, to understand an expression is to grasp the sense of that expression.[10] It is so because

> anyone who grasps the thought expressed by each of a given pair of synonymous sentences must immediately recognize one as true if he recognizes the other as true. — Ibid.: 294

Frege points out that "truth" should not be confused with quality, because truth is not a quality. This could be explained with an example. Our everyday observation reveals that sun rises in the east and sets in the west, and it is true. Here, neither we perceive the object directly nor we gather all the properties of the rays of the sun. It is simply not possible to do so, yet we are claiming it is true. How is it possible to say so? Frege explains that we could not recognize the property of an object without at the same time realizing the thought of that object, i.e. this particular object has these sorts of properties and these are to be true for that object.

---

[10] The terms "sense" and "thought" are to be understood as same in the Fregean context. Hence, both can be used interchangeably.

Frege has taken only indicative sentences for explaining the concept "truth" because an indicative sentence contains something which is not found in other sentences, namely, "assertion" and "thought". In this regard, he makes a distinction between interrogative sentence and indicative sentence. Interrogative sentences do not contain assertions whereas an indicative sentence states an assertion explaining thought.

Frege distinguishes the three following functions, namely, thinking, judging and asserting. As he puts it:

i. Apprehension of a thought — thinking
ii. Recognition of the truth of a thought — judgement
iii. Manifestation of this judgement — assertion.[11]

Consider any indicative sentence where our main concern is to know whether we can apprehend the thought from the indicative sentence or not and then we can ask if we apprehend, is it possible for us to investigate the fact what it states about? This becomes the concern of the second function. After having the appropriate investigation still we cannot claim that the sentence is either true or false. It is so because there are certain cases where it fails. For example, by seeing a flash of light we are saying that thunder is approaching but it may not be the case. So, we need the assertion which might be projected as in the form of asserting judgement. Combining all these three functions we then claim that any indicative sentence is either true or false. This is because it fulfils all the criteria of the truth condition of a proposition.

Since every sentence is endowed with thought, it possesses meaning. By the help of meaning we refer to the object that it stands for. So, from sense we are proceeding towards reference. Reference is of two sorts:

i. Direct reference
ii. Indirect reference.

---

[11] Frege 1977: 7.

In direct reference, the referent is known without any medium. In this case, we know the meaning of a word or the sense of an expression then refer to the particular object that it stands for, whereas in case of indirect reference, we frame an image which we had seen or experienced earlier, then refer to the object on the basis of that image. Frege calls indirect reference "customary sense". Indirect reference of a sentence is due to the concept which maps thoughts. So, we are able to get the truth-value of all the sentences which are having indirect references. A question is raised here, how do we know that anything whatsoever has a reference? Frege answers that when we say the word "tree", we do not intend to speak of our idea of the tree nor are we satisfied with the sense alone. Thus, we need the reference of it.

There may be cases where we understand a sentence without grasping the thought of that sentence. We grasp the thought of a sentence only when we know the meaning of the constituent parts of that sentence and their application towards the object of the phenomenal world. Hence, we know its reference. Therefore, we know its truth-value, i.e. circumstances under which the sentence will be treated as true or false.

> It is quite clear that someone might well understand either sentence, without understanding the other. And this means that we need to make a clear distinction between, on the one hand, grasping a certain thought (or concept) and, on the other hand, understanding a given sentence (or concept word). It means in fact that we have to make a clear distinction between the content of a given thought, and the sense of a particular sentence.
>
> — Bell 1996: 594

A question is raised here, how is it possible to bring together the constituent words a thought, which bring a new thought conveying more than the parts of a sentence convey?

Frege resolves this problem by analysing the "compositionality principle". The compositionality principle states that grasping a thought requires grasping of each concept which occurs as a part within that thought. He writes:

> If we look upon thoughts as composed of simple parts and take these in turn to correspond to the simple parts of sentences, we can understand how a few parts of sentences can go to make up a great multitude of sentences to which in turn they correspond a great multitude of thoughts.[12]

In a similar fashion, the sense of a proposition is determined by combining the meaning of its constituent parts through which the sentence is made up. He has also given an alternative by stating that a given thought can be constructed as a value of a certain conceptual function for certain conceptual arguments. He calls this model "function/argument model".[13] Since thoughts are complex structured, they are to be understood with certain conceptual functions and in addition to it some vivid arguments. In this connection, Wittgenstein writes, "whenever there is a complexity, functions and arguments are present" (Wittgenstein 1972: 47).

Continuing with his argument, Frege holds that the time of utterance is the part of the expression of the thought. For example, "today" is the thought to have the sense of "the present day", whereas "yesterday" could be thought to have the sense of "the day before". Thus, sense of a proposition does not move from context to references, but directly to references. As a result, we can move easily from sense to reference. Hence, we are able to get the truth-value of all the propositions.

Further, Frege argues that mere wording is not the complete expression of thought. The knowledge of certain accompanying conditions of utterances is needed for its correct apprehension, such as, in the case like pointing of fingers, hand movements, bodily gestures. It is so because the same utterance containing the word "I" will express different thoughts in diverse contexts by different

---

12 Frege 1984: 390. See Frege 1977: 55.

13 Bell 1996: 595.

speakers who uttered "I" at different times. Out of those one event may be true for someone but that may not be true for others.[14] For example, suppose a union president says "I demand that . . ." and a prisoner says "I did not do that . . .". In these two sentences the difference lies when the first one expresses about the demand of the people as a whole, the second one expresses completely a view of an individual. Some may disagree to accept that the first sentence is of the view of the group of people. They may suggest that it is completely a view of an individual but not as a whole. In this way, the uttered "I" has different thoughts in relation to different speakers in the contextual variations.

On Frege's view, reference follows from sense but they are not one and the same. From sense we can go to the reference but not inversely. The knowledge of the sense of a proposition contains in the "mode of presentation" on the basis of which we refer to something. It thus defines the "mode of applicability" of the expression. Since every sentence possesses sense and it refers to the object, from this, we can get the truth-value of the sentences.

Frege states that natural language is not well-defined and perfect. This is exhibited in the structure of its sentences. For example, the sentence, "The general will of people in a village is not same". In this sentence, how do we refer to the "general will of people" and what to refer when we say that the general will of people is not same? In this way ambiguity arises in natural language. In order to overcome the problem relating to reference failure, Frege suggests that we need a formal and a logically perfect language which he calls *Begriffsschrift.* In a formal and a logically perfect language, we find that a proposition necessarily has both sense and reference. As a result, all the propositions can be treated as either true or false.

Further, Frege explains that we cannot omit the natural language abruptly because it covers the widest as well as the largest

[14] Frege 1977: 1.

part of language. The only task to be profound is that we need to analyse it. Analysis of ordinary language can alone remove its defects. Hence, we will find the logically perfect language where each proposition can be judged as either true or false.

From the above analysis, it is observed that Frege's theory on meaning is an atomistic theory. It is so, because for him, every sentence has sense, and from sense we go to reference. Sense of a sentence is nothing but the thought of that sentence. Since every sentence has a thought, it states something about the world. Hence, we get the reference of the sentence. Reference of a sentence is same as the truth-value of that sentence. It is so because the sense of a sentence refers to the object of the world. As a result, the sentence will be confirmed that under which circumstances it will be treated as true or false. Thus, every sentence can be judged as either true or false.

If at all we call Frege a holist, then we have to take his philosophical work *Grundlagen* into consideration. In *Grundlagen*, we find the "context principle" (hereafter, CP) where he represents a particular theory in various ways. The various representations are: "Never to ask for the meaning of a word in isolation, but only in the context of a proposition", "only in a proposition have the words really a meaning", ". . . we must never try to define the meaning of a word in isolation, but only as it is used in the context of a proposition" (Frege 1980: 10, 71, 116).

Frege introduced CP much before the analysis of sense–reference distinction and the concept–object distinction. Therefore, it is doubted whether Frege gives up CP in his later period or accommodates it in the context of his overall philosophy.

Frege's main aim in *Grundlagen* is to come out with a definition of "number". For him, numbers are neither subjective nor inter-subjective, but are objective concepts. Furthermore, number is a kind of platonic object which differs from the object(s) as we find in the phenomenal world. Number can be understood in relation to objects.[15] To hold this view, he states that to ignore CP is to apprehend the claim that meanings of words are merely the subjective concepts. Subjectivity arises due to the mental pictures of individual or acts of individual mind. But if we think meaning of a word in terms of mental image then we violate the Fregean principle, i.e. the distinction between psychological and logical, the distinction between subjective and objective, which we have already discussed in the earlier sessions. For him, thinking of meaning in terms of mental image or individual mental act threatens the public nature of meaning and it disturbs the communicability and shareability among the individuals. This is because mental images vary from speaker to speaker and even vary from time to time in the case of a particular speaker. But in reality meaning is the same across the linguistic community. Therefore, we have to accept CP.

In CP, the prime objective is to establish "number" as an objective concept. It is neither a property of an object nor a mental image. So it is not subjective. The number belongs to the object only because we regard the object having that particular number. For example, consider a storybook which contains seven short stories. Here our reason for assuming the number "seven" as an object is due to our ascription of number to the object. Further, he says that a number belongs to a concept and not to an object. It is because it is the concept through which we objectify the object. Number is not a property of an object. But it is an objective concept which exists in relation to object. For example, let us consider two sentences, "The tree has one thousand leaves" and "The tree has green leaves". We can ascribe the colour green to each leaf, but we cannot ascribe the number one thousand to each of those leaves. If we call the collection of leaves foliage, even then we cannot ascribe the number one thousand to the foliage.

From the above analysis, it is asserted that we can apply the

---

[15] Here the term "object" is understood in a much wider sense which includes being as well as non-being.

notion of number to more things than the concept of colour can be applied to. For example, we can apply the concept of number not only to material objects but also to ideas, actions, judgements, etc. whereas we apply the notion of colour only to material objects.

Further, Frege points out that we should not assume that "number" is an idea. Had it been an idea, each person would have a different idea of number "1" and consequently there will be no common number to talk about. Since each idea is private to a person we cannot formulate any law of number, and thus arithmetic as an objective science would be impossible. In this connection, he explicitly states that if we accept unconscious ideas then we have to talk about unconscious number as well which is absurd, incoherent and unintelligible. Therefore, number is an objective and universal concept.

Considering the analysis of number as an objective entity, Frege vehemently expresses that each word possesses a significant meaning when it is used in the context of a sentence. For example, "There are four tables in this room". To understand the meaning of this proposition we need to understand the meaning of its each constituent word. Here, we find that the mere word "four" does not describe anything about the phenomenal world. But it makes sense when the word "four" relates to the object called table. Thus the number "four" is an objective concept. In this sense, to understand the meaning of a sentence we need the semantic contribution of each constituent word of this sentence. Holding this mechanism, we may claim that Frege is a word holist. In his theory it is clearly asserted that to understand the meaning of a word in a sentence we need to relate the meaning of other words with that word.

Our point is if Frege can at all be called a word holist, it will be only in the sense of naïve holism or the weak sense of holism that he is proposing. But we cannot claim that he is a strong holist only by considering his work on *Grundlagen* and omitting his other works. In other words, it is implausible to say that he is a holist by considering his work on *Grundlagen* independently from his other works. In his later work he proposes a few new principles such as compositionality principle, the distinction between sense and reference, and the role of thought for understanding the meaning of a proposition, where we clearly found that he is an atomist. These are the issues we have already discussed while discussing the truth-conditional approach to meaning in relation to individual sentence. If we consider all these issues as a whole then we will see Frege as a meaning atomist rather than a strong holist.

Going against CP, it is marked that words do have meaning independent of the sentences. We understand the meaning of a few sentences that we never heard before. And this is possible because we encountered the same words in other sentences earlier. On the basis of that we grasp the meaning of the sentence that we never heard before. Thus, it assumes that words not only possess their meanings in the context of a sentence but also they are capable of acquiring their meanings independently (i.e. not relating with other words).

Frege may be considered as a word holist but not as a sentence holist. According to him, the meaning of a word consists in its contribution to the meaning of the whole sentence. Therefore, he may be considered as a word holist. But if we see Frege's later works, it is noticed that he is very much concerned and interested to establish the truth-conditional approach to meaning in relation to individual sentences. For him, sense logically precedes the reference. It is the sense of a proposition through which we are able to know its referent. To Frege, reference of a sentence is same as the truth-value of that sentence because to know the reference of a sentence is to know the conditions under which the sentence will be treated as true. Thus for Frege, sentence is the unit of meaning. Of course, each constituent word of a proposition has its contribution to get the sense of a proposition. But from this it does not follow that word can be regarded as the only unit of meaning. As held by Dummett, when we explain the meaning of a sentence, our concern is on the sentence, but when we recognize the meaning of a sentence, we require the word meaning, for words are the basic constituents of a sentence.[16]

To put it more succinctly, we understand a sentence by knowing the meaning of its constituent words. But when we want to explain what it is for a word to have meaning then we need the sentence as a whole but not its parts. Thus, meaning of a word not only consists in its contribution to the meaning of the whole sentence but it also determines the truth-value of the sentence. Hence, it is stated that to grasp the meaning of a sentence is to know the truth-condition of the sentence. In this regard, Frege states that we can very well understand the meaning of a proper name by relating it to the object it stands for. This is possible when we place the proper name in a sentence and see the contribution that it makes toward the truth-value of that sentence.

Frege has taken only assertive sentences to his account for establishing that every sentence has a specific sense. The sense of a proposition is logically embedded with the proposition. For him, the sense of a proposition is same as thought of the proposition. Since he is not concerned with psychological issues, for him all the sentences state something about the facts of the world. If the sense of a sentence corresponds to the fact of the world then the sentence is true and if does not correspond to the fact of the world then the sentence will be treated as false. In this session we have argued that Frege's meaning atomism is to be seen chiefly through his truth conditional approach to meaning which is developed on the basis of sense-reference distinction.

[16] This is vividly described in Dummett 1973: 4.

3

Early Wittgenstein and Atomistic Theory of Meaning

After Frege, the next important philosophical move towards the atomistic theory of meaning was Wittgenstein's picture theory of meaning. The basic assumption of picture theory of meaning confirms to the basic tenets of meaning atomism. The objective of this chapter is to argue that picture theory of meaning offers a perspective which suggests a new way of looking at meaning atomism, i.e. meaning being viewed as picture. But the question that arises here is: why is this perspective on meaning viewed as picture embraces atomism? Wittgenstein, while formulating picture theory of meaning does not deviate from Frege. His picture theory thus takes truth-value of a proposition central to its conception of meaning. The truth-value of a proposition is to be decided in relation to individual sentences in their capacity as pictures depicting the respective states of affairs. Thus, the structure of picture theory of meaning essentially retains the Fregean structure relating to the sense of a proposition with its truth-value. However, Wittgenstein goes beyond Frege and introduces the notion of picture while talking about the sense of a proposition. The reason is that, for Frege, all propositions have both sense and reference. It is the "sense" which decides the reference of a sentence and states about how to obtain the states of affairs of the world. So for him, sense and reference are related with each other intrinsically, whereas Wittgenstein asserts that all propositions must have sense but they need not have references. It is because sense of a proposition lies in the possible description of reality. Thus for

Wittgenstein, sense is logically embedded with a proposition. It is the intrinsic property of a proposition. If it were not, then it would not be possible for us to understand a proposition without knowing its truth-value. In this sense, the sense of a proposition is same as the picture of a proposition. A proposition acquires sense when it is a picture. The picture of a proposition depicts the state of affairs of the world. The notion of picture may be thus characterized to be more comprehensive than the notion of sense in its account of meaning.

In view of the above-stated background, this session will focus on the picture theory of meaning with a view to arrive at Wittgenstein's exposition of meaning atomism. In order to undertake this, the issues that pre-eminently enter into our discussion are: the structure of a proposition, logical picture of a proposition, sign and proposition, the notion of correspondence, atomic facts, elementary proposition, and isomorphic relation between the structure of a proposition and the structure of reality. In the following pages these issues are discussed with a view to establish Wittgenstein's conception of meaning atomism as developed in his *Tractatus*.

The quest for truth arises when we talk about meaning in language. By truth we mean the logical truth which is to be understood in relation to obtaining and non-obtaining of states of affairs in the world. If we see Frege's account on truth, he holds that the word "truth" is to be explained in terms of laws of truth. Further, he remarks that one could find the truth by affirming the pictures, ideas, statements and thoughts. Considering the "picture" as one of the assertions of truth, it is said that one cannot claim a picture is true unless there is an intention behind this. So, a picture must represent something and that is about the state of affairs of the world. All the states of affairs or facts of the world can be projected in the form of assertive propositions. Thus, it is claimed that truth of a proposition is determined in relation to the correspondence of a picture that it depicts.

In the *Tractatus*, Wittgenstein clearly points out that every proposition depicts a picture. A picture is essentially related with the proposition because it is essentially the sense that a proposition expresses. The sense of a proposition deals with the objects and non-objects of the phenomenal world. So, in a sense it gives us the knowledge of what the proposition is stating about. Thus for him, a picture depicts a fact. Since it depicts a fact, it states about the existence and non-existence of objects in the world. Hence, a correspondence relation exists between the picture of a proposition and the facts of the world, i.e. what the proposition is stating about.

According to Wittgenstein, "a proposition is a picture of reality" (*Tractatus* 4.021). It is so because each proposition depicts a picture for our understanding. Picture of a proposition is logically embedded with the proposition. So, it is stated that the sense of a proposition is same as the picture of a proposition. The picture of a proposition represents the situation, i.e. what the proposition is stating about. For example, "A bird is flying". What we understand from this proposition is that there is a living creature having two legs, two wings, having feathers, not walking on the earth as men do but flying in the air. This assumes that there is a picture in our mind when someone utters the sentence "A bird is flying". As a result, we understand the meaning of the proposition. Logically speaking, in order to understand the sentence "A bird is flying" it picturizes in our mind that there is an *X* such that *X* is a bird and *X* is flying. Thus every proposition depicts a picture, i.e. what the proposition is stating about. The picture of a proposition corresponds to the facts of the world and thus all sentences can be judged as either true or false. A sentence will be treated as true if the picture of that sentence corresponds to the facts of the world. On the other hand, it turns out to be false if the picture of that proposition does not correspond to the facts of the world.

In this regard, two issues are raised here relating to the meaning of a proposition and the determination of its truth-value. They are:

1. How does meaning help to determine the truth-value of a proposition?
2. How is it possible for a hearer to understand the sense of a proposition where the constituent parts of the proposition are completely new for him?

In response to the second question, Bertrand Russell states that to know the meaning of a proposition is to understand the proposition what it states about. Hence, we have the knowledge of that proposition. On his account, we are acquiring knowledge through two ways. One is through "knowledge by acquaintance" and another is through "knowledge by description". The first one expresses that we know the meaning of a proposition when we know the meaning of its each constituent word and what they designate. It simply means that we are acquainted with the constituent words of a proposition. In this case, meaning of a proposition can be known independent of its truth-value. But this is not the case with the second one, i.e. "knowledge by description". It states that to know the meaning of a proposition is to know the conditions under which the proposition is treated as true or false. Hence, we know the meaning of a proposition through its description of the object that it states. Applying the same procedure we can understand the meaning of a proposition even though the constituent words are new to us. The description of a proposition lies in its presupposition, i.e. to describe a proposition is to know what it presupposes in a particular context. This envisages that each proposition must have logical character to satisfy the propositional attitude[1] and describes how it is used in a particular context of our discussion. With all these features there will be no hurdles for us to understand the meaning of a proposition.

In order to explain how a proposition acquires it meaning,

[1] Here, the phrase "propositional attitude" is understood as the way in which a proposition is constructed, and shows its significance when it is analysed in a language system.

Wittgenstein introduces a new theory called "picture theory of meaning". He states that "a proposition is a picture of reality: for if I understand a proposition, I know the situation that it represents" (*Tractatus* 4.021). This simply means to understand a proposition is to know what it represents or what it states about. Some problems may be encountered when we analyse the meaning of a proposition and its relation to truth conditions. For example, consider an elementary proposition where the constituent words are the proper names. The question arises, how will we get the truth-value of an elementary proposition? Mere names can neither state a fact nor any state of affairs. A name cannot be judged as either true or false. This we will be discussed when we bring the topic of elementary proposition.

Focusing on the second question further, i.e. "how do we understand a proposition which we have never come across before?" This question can be answered through an analogy. The analogy is as follows. Suppose, it is a situation where there is a small town and some people of that town are dacoits. Though a few of them are dacoits, all the people in that town maintain intimacy with each other and they have a strong feeling of togetherness. So in order to alert those dacoits of the police, the town people made some conventional signs. For instance, "green cloth means the presence of police are entering into that town", "yellow cloth means police left that town", "red cloth means someone is caught by police". No outsider can understand what those cloth stand for by simply looking at a particular colour of cloth unless someone of that town explains the significance behind a particular colour of cloth. On this analysis, we find that though all these signs are having some specific meanings, one who does not belong to that town cannot make out some sense after seeing a particular colour of cloth hanging across that town. This is possible if an outsider is having certain knowledge about the sign and its significance. In addition (s)he must have some common sense to understand certain things within its context. One can ask, what makes the outsider to make out the sense from the new sign? In a similar fashion, how is it possible for an individual to understand the sense of a proposition where the constituent words are new for him? All such problems could be resolved if we analyse Wittgenstein's picture theory of meaning.

Wittgenstein states that a proposition must be a picture of the situation that it describes no matter whether it exists or does not exist in the phenomenal world. Again, to know the sense of a proposition means to know the situation that it describes. In this regard, he says that just by looking at a proposition, I can tell what situation it describes. I can "read off" from the proposition itself, even if the proposition is quite new to me and no one has explained its sense to me[2] (Pitcher 1972: 77). This is possible because for him, a proposition shows its sense but does not state its sense (*Tractatus* 4.022). Thus, sense is the intrinsic property of a proposition.

In the picture theory of meaning it is stated that every proposition depicts a picture. Here, Wittgenstein does not mean the ordinary kind of picture, rather it is a "logical picture" or the spatial picture of the situation that a proposition describes. In order to have a logical picture of a proposition it must satisfy three features. These are:

1. There must be one to one correspondence between the thing and its picture.
2. Every feature of the real object must be found with the picture of that object.
3. Components of real object must be same as the components of the picture of that object.

Since each proposition depicts a picture and the picture represents a situation what the proposition describes, from this it is asserted that every proposition represents a fact or a state of affairs of the world. In this sense, Wittgenstein expresses that a

[2] This is explained in *Tractatus* 4.021.

proposition is a model of the situation. Thus for him, "A proposition is a model of reality as we imagine it" (*Tractatus* 4.01). But there are cases where propositions are constituted with proper names. In this case propositions do not describe the state of affairs of the world. So question arises, how can we claim that all the propositions are regarded as model of reality? Further, how is it possible that a series of mere names that are the constituent parts of a proposition can describe a fact or a state of affairs and how can this sort of proposition be treated as either true or false?

Wittgenstein replies that one name stands for one thing, another for another thing, and they are combined with one another. In this way the whole group — like a *tableau vivant* — presents a state of affairs (*Tractatus* 4.0311). In addition to this, he states that only acts can express a sense, a set of names cannot (*Tractatus* 3.142).

Here, the question arises, how is it that a picture represents a situation? Wittgenstein answers that what constitutes a picture is that its elements are related to one another in a different way (*Tractatus* 2.14). A picture is a fact because the fact that the elements of a picture are related to one another in a determinate way represents that things are related to one another in a same way (*Tractatus* 2.15). Hence, each picture represents a situation that the proposition describes.

Like a picture, a propositional sign is also a fact because "what constitutes a propositional sign is that in it its elements (the words) stand in a determinate relation to one another" (*Tractatus* 3.14). A question is raised here, what does a propositional sign depict? Wittgenstein's answer is that the elements of a propositional sign are related in such a manner that they represent the structure of a proposition. Structure of a proposition explains the situation that the proposition describes when it abides by the pictorial form. In this connection, Wittgenstein remarks that the configuration of objects in a situation corresponds to the configuration of simple signs in the propositional sign (*Tractatus* 3.12). A proposition is not same as a picture but it represents the picture of a situation. It is because a proposition has a particular reference, it describes a state of affairs of the world and further, it maps a definite situation that the proposition expresses, whereas the picture by itself is a described phenomenon. Again, a proposition describes a fact whereas the picture is itself a description of that fact. There are a few more differences between a proposition and the picture of a proposition. A picture does not state anything unless we relate it to the objects of the world. On the other hand, a proposition states something about the phenomenal world. A picture does not assert the things necessarily which are found in the empirical world, but in case of a proposition, it asserts something which is found in the phenomenal world and it states what is the case if it is true.

The pictorial relationship consists of the correlation between the elements of the picture and the object they denote (*Tractatus* 2.1514). On Wittgenstein's account, a proposition is a picture of a situation. Here, what he means is that, it is a definite representational picture which expresses a certain determinate situation. Further, he claims that the picture of a determinate situation of a proposition is a logical one. Every proposition depicts a picture which is same as every proposition has a perfectly determinate sense. The method of the projection of a sentence is to think of the sense of a proposition. He states that a proposition is a picture of a situation, which one can immediately see from looking at or hearing the proposition what the situation it describes. In his words, "A proposition states something only in so far as it is a picture" (*Tractatus* 4.03(4)). In this regard, a question is raised here, how can a proposition say something just by virtue of being a picture?

A proposition asserts something whereas a picture does not. No one can deny that a proposition depicts a picture. At best, an individual can only deny the picture by saying that it is not the right one. But he cannot deny the picture as such. It is noted that a picture can be used to assert something but it itself does not assert anything. Being a picture it states whether it agrees with the reality or not. The agreement and disagreement with reality provide the basis for a proposition to be claimed as either true or false. In this connection, Wittgenstein holds the view that there are differences existing between a proposition and the picture of a proposition. A proposition communicates a situation to us and so it is essentially connected with the situation. This connection is precisely a logical connection between the picture of a proposition and the proposition itself. In this regard, Wittgenstein states that a proposition shows how things stand if it is true and it also says that they do so (*Tractatus* 4.022(2)). Here, he simply means that a proposition is true when it corresponds with the state of affairs existing in the phenomenal world. Hence, a proposition states something only in so far as it is a picture (*Tractatus* 4.03(4)).

The picture of a proposition is same as the sense of a proposition, and also it is same with the thought of a proposition. On this occasion, Wittgenstein viewed that "a logical picture of facts is a thought" (*Tractatus* 3). In a proposition thought finds an expression that can be perceived by the senses (*Tractatus* 3.1). In a proposition a thought can be expressed in such a way that elements of the propositional sign correspond to the objects of the thought (*Tractatus* 3.2). The totality of true thoughts is a picture of the world (*Tractatus* 3.01). A state of affairs is thinkable; what this means is that we can picture it to ourselves (*Tractatus* 3.001). Thought can be expressed through language. It is the picture which makes a link between thought and language. A picture becomes meaningful as it is incorporated into the intentional situation. Thus it is viewed that a picture is a model of reality (*Tractatus* 2.12). Picture of a proposition cannot be separated from the content and context of a proposition. It is so because by the help of content picture gets its life. A question is raised here, what is that a proposition represents if it is a picture? Wittgenstein viewed that a proposition represents a situation or a state of affairs when it is a picture. From this we can assert whether a proposition is to be called either true or false. A proposition is to be judged as true when the picture of a proposition correctly matches with the state of affairs of the world and it turns out to be false if it does not correctly match with the state of affairs of the world. Thus, Wittgenstein eloquently expresses that a person understands a proposition means he or she knows what is the case if it is true.

In this connection, Wittgenstein shows the difference between meaning of a name and meaning of a proposition. A name does not have meaning if it does not correspond to object. This is so because meaning of a name is the object it names. On the contrary, there are cases where propositions have meaning but they do not correspond to any state of affairs of the world. Thus Wittgenstein stated that "names have meaning and the propositions have sense".[3]

Sense of a proposition is same as the thought of that proposition. On this account Frege aptly expresses that "the thought is not the subjective performance of thinking but its objective content, which is capable of being the common property of several thinkers" (Frege 1952: 62). Here, Frege means that though thoughts on a particular fact vary from person to person yet there are some objectivities involved with it to understand the fact as the same, which Frege calls the objectivity of thought. So for him, thought of a sentence is objective and eternal. Considering this analysis it is marked that the sense of a proposition is thus a strange kind of objective entity which is apprehended by the several speaker's mind. So every sentence forms some kind of pictures in our mind. As a result we understand the situation what the sentence is stating about. If the situation correctly maps with the stating of fact then the sentence is true and if does not correctly map then it is false. Here, Wittgenstein states that the sense of a proposition is the situation it describes. The situation is itself a picture. This picture is a kind of logical picture. In his words, "What a picture represents is its sense" (*Tractatus* 2.221).

Sense of a proposition depicts or represents the picture of a

[3] For more details please see Wittgenstein 1979: 94.

situation and that situation must agree with the reality to claim the proposition as true. Here, the question arises if it is so then what about false proposition? Do we hold the view that false proposition represents a false picture and hence the false picture of a proposition is contentless? Furthermore, since false propositions do not describe any situation or state of affairs should we say that all false propositions make no sense?

Wittgenstein replies to this question by introducing a new concept called "possible situation" where he makes a link between the possible situation and the existent and non-existent state of affairs of the world. The existent state of affairs is a positive fact whereas the non-existent state of affairs is a negative fact. In his words, the existent and non-existent state of affairs of the world is reality (*Tractatus* 2.06). For him, state of affairs is atomic because it corresponds to the elementary proposition. Therefore, elementary propositions are also atomic. Elementary propositions cannot be divided further into more basic propositions. They deal with objects of the world directly. In a similar fashion state of affairs of the world cannot be reduced to any further basic state of affairs of the world.

Names are the constituent parts of an elementary proposition. All names refer to the objects of the world. Since elementary propositions assert the existence of state of affairs, they correspond to the objects of the world. This is so because all the state of affairs consists of objects only. Hence, all propositions have truth-value. Therefore, Wittgenstein states that every proposition is essentially either true or false. If the proposition corresponds to the fact that it describes then the proposition is judged as true. On the contrary, if the proposition does not correspond to the fact it is judged as false. So truth or falsity of a proposition is determined from the sense of a proposition. Sense is logically embedded with the proposition. Thus every sentence has a sense, i.e. what it expresses.

Considering an elementary proposition *aRb* and its negation ~ *aRb*, it is stated that these two propositions have opposite sense.

To say, the state of affairs *aRb* exists implies if *a* does bear the relation R to *b* then *aRb* is true and ~ *aRb* is false. In this connection, Wittgenstein states that "names are like points, propositions like arrows and they have sense" (*Tractatus* 3.144). This is so because a name like *a*, or *b*, is static. It does not move. It refers to certain object whereas proposition moves. The proposition *aRb* moves from *a* to *b*. Thus a proposition is a truth function of elementary proposition.

Picture Theory of Meaning

Wittgenstein in his picture theory of meaning states that all genuine propositions are truth functions of elementary propositions. On this account, Anscombe writes that the picture theory does not permit any function of propositions other than truth functions. Indeed, we should not regard Wittgenstein's theory of proposition as a synthesis of a picture theory of truth functions; his picture theory and theory of truth functions are one and the same (Anscombe 1971: 81). The essence of the truth functions of a proposition states that the world divides into atomic facts. There are no irreducible general facts. So, all general facts can be reduced to atomic facts. Hence, all propositions state about the atomic facts of the world. As a result, it corresponds to the objects of the world. Therefore, all propositions can have truth-value. If a proposition does not correspond to the facts of the world then that proposition is false. On the contrary, if a proposition corresponds to the facts of the world then it is true.

A complex situation is described by a truth function of elementary propositions. An elementary proposition describes the state of affairs which makes up a complex situation, so the only terms that could denote whatever that is supposed to bind the state of affairs together the truth functional operators, the so-called logical constants (Pitcher 1972: 70). Logically speaking, two elementary propositions are neither contradictory nor contrary to each other. It is so because elementary proposition expresses the state of affairs of the world. Since states of affairs are independent from each other it entails that a particular elementary proposition is neither reduced to another nor is deduced from another. In this connection, Wittgenstein states that "from the existence or non-existence of one state of affairs it is impossible to infer the existence or non-existence of another" (*Tractatus* 2.062).

Let us consider two different elementary propositions *Fa* and *Ga*. We cannot deduce one from the other without adding any one of the premises, "If *Fa* then *Ga*" or "All *Fa* are *Ga*". These two propositions are respectively symbolized as: $Fa \rightarrow Ga$ and $(\forall a)\ (Fa \rightarrow Ga)$. These alternative premises help in deducing an elementary proposition from another, i.e. either from *Fa* to *Ga* or from *Ga* to *Fa*. Without these two alternative premises we are unable to deduce one proposition from the other. It is marked that there is no possibility to infer the existence of one situation from the existence of another which is entirely different. So the elementary propositions are logically independent from each other. The question arises, why there has to be an elementary proposition? Wittgenstein replies that elementary propositions depict the primitive states of affairs which are constituted by the combination of simple objects. With this, by the help of referential theory or so-called correspondence theory we can get the truth-value of a proposition. Further, we put a question, why there has to be a simple object? Wittgenstein answers that it is so because "objects are simple" (*Tractatus* 2.02).

In fact, Frege states that every well-formed proposition must have a sense and reference. From sense we can go to the reference. Holding this view, Wittgenstein aptly expresses that "every possible proposition is well-formed, and if it does not make sense, this can only come of our not having supplied any reference for some of its component parts" (Anscombe 1971: 68). The sense of a proposition depicts what is the case and differentiates it from what is not the case. So a proposition states about the existence and non-existence of the situation where each situation corroborates with some elements and these elements are related with the objects of the world. Hence, each situation refers to the object of the world for explaining what the case is and what the case is not. Therefore, all sentences can be judged as either true or false. In this way sentences deal with the situations and this implies that they express about the states of affairs of the world.

Again, each proposition represents a situation. That situation can give rise to the correct or incorrect picture of a proposition. The elements of a proposition are the basic ingredients which are arranged in a logical and sequential manner in a proposition. The way in which the elements are combined together provides a logical picture. This is what Wittgenstein calls the structure of picture. So every picture has a structure. But the structure of a picture and the picture itself are not identical with each other. It is so because the picture consists of a structure and it includes the pictorial relationship. The pictorial relationship states about the objects of the phenomenal world whereas the structure of a picture shows how the elements are concatenated in the picture. In this connection, Wittgenstein states that the concatenation of the elements in a picture is called the structure of the picture. Each proposition depicts a picture. The picture represents a fact. Since it represents a fact, all the propositions can be judged as either true or false. The proposition will be true if the picture of the proposition corresponds to the facts of the world and it will be turned out to be false when the picture of a proposition does not correspond to the facts of the world.

According to Wittgenstein,

> There must be something identical in a picture and what it depicts to enable the one to be a picture of the other at all. What a picture must have in common with reality, in order to be able to depict it — correctly or incorrectly — in the way it does, is its pictorial form.
>
> — *Tractatus* 2.161, 2.17

Here, Wittgenstein states that there must exist one-to-one relation between the elements of a picture and the objects of a fact on the ground that each fact depicts a picture. On this consideration, it is asserted that since each proposition depicts a picture it states about the objects of the reality. Further he states:

> The elements of the picture must be capable of some combination with each other in a pattern corresponding to the relationship of the elements of what is picture. — Kenny 1973: 57

From this it is understood that every picture represents a possible state of affairs and it refers to the existence and non-existence of objects of the world. A picture will be considered true if it agrees with the reality and false if it does not agree with the reality. A proposition which depicts a picture can neither be affirmed as true nor as false unless it pictures the reality. It is so because it is the elementary proposition which describes about the reality presented in a pictorial form to claim that whether the proposition is true or false. Hence, all elementary propositions can be treated as either true or false on the basis of their logical pictures. It is pointed out that the sense of a proposition is same as the thought of a proposition. This is because the thought of a proposition states about the facts or state of affairs of the world. The proposition is true, if the thought which is expressed by the proposition corresponds to the facts of the world and if it does not correspond to the facts of the world then it is false. Hence, thought is the logical picture of a fact.

A question is raised here, if a picture is a combination of elements then what the elements of a thought? Wittgenstein replies, "I don't know what the constituents of a thought are, but I know that it must have such constituents which correspond to the words of language" (Kenny 1973: 58). Further, he states that only possible states of affairs can be thought of. The totality of true thoughts is the picture of the world. Since any picture needs to be compared with reality to tell whether it is correct or not, there cannot be a thought whose truth is recognizable from the thought itself. Hence, no thought can be considered as an a priori truth (*Tractatus* 3.01-05). Thought is a bridge which links between the propositions on one hand, and the states of affairs on the other hand. Thus, all the propositions are essentially either true or false.

Wittgenstein states that a proposition is a picture, and it depicts the facts that it describes (Kenny 1973: 62). In order to establish this, i.e. "a proposition is a picture of the fact" he has given the following arguments.

a. *A proposition is essentially composite*: A proposition is the result of the combination of a string of words conveying a specific meaning. But any combination of words does not constitute a sentence. For example, "cow flies hinge duster". In this sentence all the constituent words are not used in a determinate way. So it does not convey any specific meaning. In this regard, Wittgenstein states that "a mere set of names cannot express a sense" (*Notebooks* 105). It is marked that a proposition unlike a name must have parts and the parts of a sentence must have a specific meaning in the context of a sentence. We regard meaning of a proposition is same as the sense of a proposition and also it is same with the picture of a proposition. From this, we can infer that every sentence depicts a picture and sentences are essentially composite in their nature.

b. *The correlation of the elements of a proposition*: The correlation of the elements of a proposition should be affixed in an appropriate way; otherwise it does not convey any specific meaning. For example, "Horse duster green click is circle". This sentence does not possess any specific meaning because the elements of the proposition are not correlated with each other in a determinate way. A proposition however is not just a set of names; in addition to that we have to correlate the names with objects. We have to make a relationship between the names in a proposition and the objects that they designate.[4]

c. *Non-arbitrary representation of a proposition*: A proposition represents the situation that it describes. The correlation of names and objects expressed in a proposition is arbitrary

[4] This idea has borrowed from Kenny 1973: 65.

and thus this relationship is considered to be conventional. Once a convention is established we do not need any further convention to justify it. This is how it is possible to understand a proposition which has not been previously heard.

d. *The intrinsic relation between the proposition and the situation it describes*: Since a proposition depicts a situation, it must intrinsically and essentially link with the proposition. The linkage between the proposition and the situation it describes is a logical one, i.e. the logical picture. Every proposition endowed with two features, essential and accidental. Accidental features are resulted from the arbitrary conventions of the particular language to which it belongs whereas the essential features are those without which propositions could not express their sense (*Tractatus* 3.34). The relation between the proposition and the situation is neither causal nor reliant but an internal one. In this regard, Wittgenstein states that internal relation is one which is unexplainable. What we explain is the relation between the two, i.e. between the proposition and the situation that it describes. But the internal relation as such however we explain it cannot be an accurate and exact explanation. Hence, our explanation of it will be approximate. In this sense, it is stated that though the internal relation is known to the speaker, it is independent from the speaker. This is because the internal relation exists between the two objects only. Thus, it is asserted that the internal and essential property of a proposition is same as the logical structure of a proposition. Hence, a proposition describes the reality through its internal properties (*Tractatus* 4.023).

e. *The internal relation between the proposition and the situation can be shown but cannot be stated*: Something can be said if and only if the hearer could grasp the content of what it is being stated. From this, it is asserted that internal relation is one that cannot be stated. This is so because the internal relationship between a proposition and the situation though made by the individual, the individual is independent from it. In a sense, the internal relationship is not possessed by the individual. It confines to the objects only. Bringing the distinction between two occurrences "showing" and "stating", Wittgenstein explains that stating consists in "referring" and "describing", and they are not found in the case of an internal relation between the proposition and the situation that it describes, whereas showing consists in "representing" and "arranging", and this expounds the internal relation between the proposition and the situation that it describes. Further, in the case of "showing" both representing and arranging occur simultaneously, whereas in the case of "stating", describing follows from referring and vice versa. From this, it is argued that the internal relation between a proposition and the situation that it describes can be shown only, but cannot be stated. Hence, a proposition represents a particular situation.

f. *Truth-value of a sentence is determined from the process of comparison between the proposition and the reality*: There is no way of finding out from the proposition itself whether it is true or false. In order to get the truth-value of a proposition we must compare the proposition with the reality. It is assumed that unless a proposition were a picture we would not know where to link it to the world in order to verify the proposition (*Notebooks* 8). Thus, if a proposition corresponds to the reality then it is true and if does not correspond to the reality then it is false.

g. *Propositions exist independent of reality*: Each proposition does not necessarily express the actual state of affairs but they may state the possible states of affairs. Though a proposition expresses a state of affairs which is about the world yet they are not one and the same. A reality consists of existing and non-existing states of affairs. Every proposition depicts a picture. A picture represents something independently of its truth or falsity. More to say, a proposition acquires a sense when it depicts a picture. The mere proposition which is the outcome of the concatenation of certain words does not state anything. It states when we make a relation between the sense of a proposition or the picture of a proposition with the facts or state of affairs of the world.

h. *No proposition is true a priori*: A proposition is true a priori when the truth of that proposition is recognized independent of reality. According to Wittgenstein this is impalpable and implausible. It is so because every proposition expresses a state of affairs. The truth-value of a proposition is determined when there will be a comparison between the proposition and the state of affairs of the world that the proposition is stating about. In this regard, Wittgenstein states that "in order for a proposition to be capable of being true it must also be capable of being false" (*Notebooks* 55). All the genuine propositions are contingent propositions. The logical propositions which are counted as a priori can be seen to be true symbols alone, this shows they are only propositions by courtesy (*Notebooks* 127). So, they are not counted as propositions in true sense of the term.

Assume a situation where someone said something but we do not understand what (s)he is talking about. So we ask her/him, "what do you mean by that?". Then (s)he explains the same thing in ordinary terms, so that we understand what (s)he is speaking about. At last we may say "Oh! You mean that thing". Here, when we understood what (s)he has said, we picturize something in our mind. In this connection, Wittgenstein states that "a logical picture of facts is a thought" (*Tractatus* 3). A state of affairs is thinkable: what this means is that we can picturize the state of affairs into ourselves (*Tractatus* 3.001). Hence, the totality of true thoughts is a picture of the world (*Tractatus* 3.01). Thinking is quite comparable to the drawing of pictures (*Philosophical Grammar* 163). Thinking on a fact is not same as picturizing that fact. A picture provides a good allegory for understanding thinking. In a proposition, a thought finds an expression that can be perceived by the senses (*Tractatus* 3.1). A thought can be expressed in a proposition in such a manner that the elements of the propositional sign correspond to the objects of the thought. It is the picture which brings the possible differences between the thought and the language. Thus it is stated that "language is a picturing, thinking is a language, and thinking is a picturing" (Genova 1995: 66). To understand a proposition means to know the facts what it states about. According to Wittgenstein, picture is identified with the model. Thus for him, to say a proposition is a picture of reality is same as a proposition is a model of reality. Hence, a picture is a model of reality (*Tractatus* 2.12). A model envisages the structural framework of a state of affairs where the state of affairs is the representation of a proposition.

To use a sentence involves imagining something for every word. Each word has its own significance in the language. There are signs which may represent in the form of words having a particular meaning. If it were not, then what for the arrow sign "→" stands for? We cannot claim that it is just a dead line on a paper because it carries something with it, i.e. "meaning". Thus, it has a particular significance in a contextual paradigm. It is the meaning which states that we have to go ahead in a particular direction in which way the arrow is marked. From this, it is assumed that the picture on its own has no longer reached out to the reality unless we make a link between the picture and what it represents. It is the meaning which makes the picture alive.

> It is no more essential to the understanding of a proposition that one should imagine anything in connection with it but rather one should make a sketch from it. — *Philosophical Investigations* 396

Every proposition depicts a picture. To ask whether the picture maps the state of affairs of the world is to look for its truth-value.

In this regard, Wittgenstein states that we have to apply the picture to the reality. If it corresponds to the reality then the proposition is true and if does not correspond to the reality then it is false. In the process of determining the truth-value of a proposition we find there is a difference between the determination of the sense of a proposition and the employment of the sense of a proposition. To determine the sense of a proposition we need the meaning of its constituent parts and what they refer to, whereas to employ the sense of a proposition we require its picture to map the reality.

In the *Tractatus*, Wittgenstein aptly expresses that "sense" is the logical content of a proposition. It lies in the possible description of reality. The reality of a proposition is explained through two ways:

i. by explaining sense, and
ii. by explaining the truth condition.

Sense reflects the picture in a proposition. The proposition will be true if the sense of a proposition agrees with reality and if it does not agree with the reality then it will be treated as false. Thus, "A proposition is a picture of reality" (*Tractatus* 4.12). By the help of "explication" we can bring out the truth condition of a proposition. Wittgenstein states that propositions can be judged as either true or false because they are endowed with "thoughts" and they are about the world. Thus, he conceives that we cannot imagine a sentence without its truth condition.

Wittgenstein prescribes two principles through which we can travel from "sense" to "reference". They are:

i. principle of applicability, and
ii. principle of identity.

To know the sense of a proposition is to know "where to apply" it. This encompasses the first principle, i.e. the principle of applicability. Once we know "where to apply", we are capable of knowing "what to apply". As a result, we will identify the corresponding object. This envisages the second principle, i.e.

"principle of identity". Hence, we are able to determine the truth-value of a proposition. In this way "sense" and "truth-value" of a proposition are internally and intrinsically related with each other.

Further, Wittgenstein states that all propositions are made about the world. This is so because the constituent words of a proposition which are in the form of "names" have one-to-one correspondence with the objects of the world. So necessarily a proposition is either true or false. The proposition will be true if the names in it are corresponding to the object named, otherwise false. The "sense" of a proposition is logically embedded with the structure of a proposition. Thus, sense is the mirror of the structure of a proposition. The most important feature of "sense" is "manifestibility" which conveys that the sense of a proposition manifests itself when it is used in our language. In order to establish this, he has given two criteria:

1. logical form of the proposition, and
2. logical form of the world.

The first one expresses about the "structure" or "the form of a proposition" whereas the second one expresses about the reality which is the exact copy of a situation. He makes it clear by stating that there is no structure of the world if there is no logical structure of the proposition. It is so because the logical structure of a proposition is the mirror of the world. The logical structure of a proposition states about the logical picture of a situation which is about the world. In this connection, Wittgenstein states that truth and falsity do not arise if the proposition does not express about the world.

To know the "sense" of a proposition is to know the essence of that proposition which includes both "picture" and "structure" of that proposition. In his view, if we do not accept that proposition is a picture of reality then we cannot express how a proposition acquires its sense. When the sense of a proposition agrees with reality the proposition will be treated as true and if the sense of a proposition does not agree with the reality then the proposition will be treated as false. Thus, the truth-value of a proposition is determined by the sense of that proposition. Hence, understanding a proposition requires to know what the case is if it is true.

In the *Tractatus* it is stated that a proposition will be true if it corresponds to a fact or a state of affairs of the world and there must be a relation between the fact and the sense of a proposition. In this connection, Wittgenstein expresses that a proposition is a picture of reality. For establishing this he has described some measures as follows:

1. A proposition is a picture of situation.
2. A proposition states something about the phenomenal world.
3. A proposition expresses something only in so far as it is a picture.[5]
4. A proposition communicates a situation to us, and so, it must be essentially connected with the situation.[6]
5. The connection between a proposition and the situation is a logical connection that may be called as logical picture of a proposition.[7]

These five measures help to assert that a proposition is a picture of the reality. Since it is so, it states about the facts of the world. Therefore, every sentence can be judged as either true or false.

It is viewed that every proposition has a specific content. Since each proposition possesses a specific content, it expresses something definite and indubitable, and this is possible due to the logical picture of a proposition. Hence, every proposition depicts a logical picture. The logical picture of a proposition states about the world. Here, we find there is a correspondence between the logical picture of a proposition and the facts of the world. Therefore, every

[5] *Tractatus Logico-Philosophicus* 4.03(4).

[6] Ibid. 4.03(2).

[7] Ibid. 4.03(3).

proposition is essentially either true or false. A proposition is true when the sense of a proposition or a so-called logical picture of a proposition agrees with the reality. On the other hand, a proposition is false when the sense of a proposition does not agree with the reality. Thus, language is a part of the world.

According to Wittgenstein, the ordinary words which are in the form of "names" stand one-to-one relation with objects. So a proposition is necessarily either true or false. It will be true if the names in it are related in a way corresponding to the relations of the objects named. For him, to give the essence of a proposition means to give the essence of the world.[8] The essence of a proposition is derived from the spatial arrangement of objects within a fact, which the proposition expresses. Thus, language is a part of the world and the propositions are themselves facts. There are no negative facts because facts are the results of combination of objects. If a proposition is true then there is a corresponding fact existed to it and, if there is no corresponding fact then it is regarded as false. Hence, a proposition is essentially either true or false.

On the above analysis, it is viewed that a proposition acquires sense when it depicts a picture. This picture is not a kind of ordinary picture rather it is a spatial or logical picture. A proposition depicts a picture means it states about the existing and non-existing states of affairs of the world. The picture itself cannot be counted as either true or false; it is the proposition which depicts the picture as either true or false. A proposition is true when the picture what it depicts corresponds with the reality and it turns out to be false when the picture does not correspond with the reality. Thus, a proposition is true or false completely depends on the nature of its own analysis, i.e. through the mechanism of "truth-functional" system of logic. Each proposition can be shown to be essentially either true or false. This makes it evident that the analysis of propositions is to be achieved by the truth-functional system of logic.

---

[8] This notion is described by Wittgenstein in his book *Tractatus*, where he has intended to describe how the proposition deals with the world.

4

Logical Positivistism and Atomistic Theory of Meaning

THE MOST important and significant issue regarding meaning is: How do we understand the meaning of a proposition? In other words, what sorts of mechanism are involved for acquiring the meaning of a proposition? As we have stated in the previous chapters, the meaning of a proposition is inseparably related to its truth-value of what that proposition asserts. In this connection, Wittgenstein in his "picture theory of meaning" viewed that "meaning" and "truth conditions" are so related with each other that one cannot imagine a proposition without its truth condition.

In our earlier discussion on the meaning of a proposition, we have argued that the idea of meaning essentially includes the idea of logical bivalence as its essential component. This is because if we know the meaning of a proposition then we know the situations or circumstances where the proposition will be judged as true or false. Hence, the relation between the meaning of a proposition and its truth-value appears to be identical in the sense of having a "tight-knit-association". In this regard, Wittgenstein emphatically expressed that there is no indeterminacy of sense of a proposition. All the propositions must have sense because sense is the logical and intrinsic property of a proposition. Further, he said that sense is the criterion through which we determine the reference. In his view, to know the sense of a proposition means to know the conditions where the sentence is to be applied and where it is not.

In other words, we are able to know the conditions under which the proposition will be true and false. The view expressed here corresponds to logical positivist's verifiability theory of meaning. According to them, the sense of a proposition is the method of its verification.[1] It is the verifiability theory which determines the truth-value of a proposition. Further, logical positivists assert that though meaning of a proposition is determined by its constituent words and the grammatical rules, in some cases these principles are not enough or sufficient to acquire the meaning of a proposition. For example, suppose a person says "His dog is very crazy", or "Motion is restless". In this case to understand the propositions it is not enough for us to know the meaning of its constituent words and the grammatical rules through which the proposition is governed, rather we should know the situations where the sentence is to be applied and where it is not. In other words, under which circumstances the proposition will be treated as true and under which circumstances the sentence will be treated as false. Here, the individual proposition matters in order to account for its truth-value. It does not require any further sentences to get its truth-value. Thus, it satisfies the atomistic theory of meaning, i.e. meaning of a proposition is understood without relating it with other propositions.

According to the logical positivists, the reason for introducing the verifiability theory is:

a. All the statements in a language are divided into two sorts, analytic and synthetic,

b. meaning of a statement would be assimilated through our observational sense-data or experiences, and

c. meaning of a statement is determined by the verifiability criterion.

---

[1] This is pointed out by Wittgenstein in his *Philosophical Remarks*, when he had a conversation with Schlick and Waismann, regarding the issue of verifiability theory of meaning. See Munitz 1981: 228.

Logical positivists' theory of meaning can be claimed to be a formulation of atomistic theory of meaning. This view can be seen in continuation to Frege and Early Wittgenstein's approaches to meaning. This is because logical positivists hold the same view as Frege and early Wittgenstein ascribe, i.e. the meaning of a proposition is determined by its truth-value. This prescription on meaning is atomistic because it holds that the meaning of a proposition can be determined in isolation from the rest of the propositions in a language. Thus, meaning of a sentence does not require any further propositions or its understanding. It is self-sufficient and self-evident to convey its meaning independently from other propositions. This is so because the main concern of meaning, as argued here, is about the facts or states of affairs of the world. The proposition which states about facts or states of affairs of the world will be regarded as true when the meaning of the proposition corresponds to the facts of the world, and if it does not, then the proposition will be treated as false.

Logical positivism accepts a full-blooded version of this view of meaning. Its concern for empirical knowledge exerts considerable influence on its view on meaning. Meaning is thus viewed in experiential term. Accordingly, logical positivists argue that a proposition will be meaningful if it is either true or false, and truth or falsity will be decided in the light of sense-experience. In this connection, they introduced verifiability as a criterion of meaning through which they tried to establish the inseparable connection between meaning and sense-experience. According to them, the sense of a proposition means to know the method of its verification. While perusing this they considered only individual propositions for verification through which meaning of a sentence under consideration is established. It is through verifiability criterion one confirms whether the meaning of a proposition matches correctly with the facts of the world or not. Accordingly, the truth-value of the proposition is decided. If a proposition does not have any truth-value it is rendered meaningless.

On this ground, logical positivists made a claim that a sentence is meaningful if and only if what it expresses is either analytic or empirically verifiable. From this it is held that to know the meaning of a proposition is to know its truth-value. Hence, for a statement not having truth-value means it is regarded as meaningless statement. On this ground, they criticized Kant's synthetic–a priori statements. First of all, a statement cannot be both synthetic and a priori. It is a contradiction in terms. Here, logical positivists claim that synthetic–a priori statements do not deal with the facts or states of affairs of the phenomenal world, rather they deal with the metaphysical entities which cannot be verified empirically by the help of our observational experiences. Further, it gives us the knowledge about the metaphysical reality which transcends our experience all together. Thus, synthetic–a priori statements are meaningless.

Elimination of Metaphysics

According to the view of logical positivists, metaphysical statements are meaningless because they are cognitively meaningless. They transcend the world of science and common sense. Since they do not deal with the facts of the empirical world they cannot be determined as either true or false in the light of sense experience. Thus, they lack truth-value. The statements which transcend the limits of possible sense experiences cannot have any literal significance.

The charge made against metaphysicians is not that they attempt to employ the understanding in a field where it cannot be profitably ventured but they produce statements which fail to confirm to the conditions under which a statement can be literally significant. Thus, logical positivists hold the view that through the verifiability criterion one can verify truth or falsity of a statement. Hence, the meaningfulness of a statement will be determined without any doubt. In other words, a statement is factually significant to any given person if and only if he knows how to verify the statement in question.

On the basis of the above consideration, logical positivists said that all metaphysical assertions are nonsensical because they do not convey anything about the facts of the world. They are not also a priori. So a metaphysical statement is one which purports to express a genuine proposition but in fact expresses neither a tautology nor an empirical hypothesis. The problem which lies with metaphysicians is that they fail to see the relation between the statement and what it states about. This is because metaphysicians are misled by a superficial grammatical feature of the language. Logical positivists argue that the grammatical form of language hides its logical form. Let us consider the two following sentences as an example. "Unicorns are fictitious" and "Dogs are faithful".[2] Here, both the sentences are of same grammatical form but differ in their logical form. The analysis of the two sentences is as follows. Dogs must exist in order to have the property of being faithful. But the problem arises with the unicorn. Unless unicorn exists the property of being fictitious will not exist. Now to state that fictitious objects have a special non-empirical mode of real being is devoid of all literal significance. Hence, the truth-value of the first proposition cannot be determined. Therefore, it is a meaningless proposition. Metaphysical propositions are of the same nature whose truth-value cannot be determined and thus they can be ruled out from being called meaningful statements of a language.

According to logical positivists, a proposition is factually significant when a person knows how to verify the proposition. To verify a proposition means to know the observations under which the proposition is said to be true or false. In this respect, Waismann states that "a person who utters a proposition must know under what conditions the proposition is to be called true or false; if he is not able to specify that, he also does not know what he has said" (Hanfling 1981: 27). Adding to it, he states that to understand a proposition means to know how things stand, i.e. what the proposition is about. Thus, for logical positivists, the

---

[2] This example is taken from Ayer 1976. Also see Ammerman 1965: 119.

principle of verification is the criterion for determining the literal meaning of a proposition.

To say that a proposition is meaningful is to say that it is empirically verifiable. The criterion of verifiability is not to be used as a method for determining the actual truth or falsity of a statement rather it is used for determining the necessary conditions for inquiring into truth, namely, whether a particular statement has a literal meaning or not. Thus, the criterion of truth and falsity of a proposition is dependent on the conditions under which certain data are present or not.

In support this view, Schlick states that the meaning of a statement is the method of its verification.[3] Continuing his argument he expresses that if we do not know what are the observational sensory experiences to be met in order to judge whether a statement is true or false then the statement will be regarded as a pseudo statement. Thus, it is unverifiable and therefore meaningless.

The Criterion of Meaningfulness

The meaning of an expression or a proposition is associated with the cognitive use of language which implies whether a proposition is true or false, i.e. a proposition must have a truth-value. The criterion of meaningfulness is associated with the criterion of verifiability. The verifiability criterion determines the truth-value of a sentence by providing the necessary conditions under which the statement can be verified. As A.J. Ayer points out:

> The principle of verification is supposed to furnish a criterion by which it can be determined whether or not a sentence is literally meaningful. A simple way to formulate it would be to say that a sentence had literal meaning if and only if the proposition it expressed was either analytic or empirically verifiable.
>
> —Ayer 1976: 7

[3] Schlick 1981: 5.

According to Schlick, if a person knows the meaning of a proposition he will be able to indicate the relevant circumstances under which it would be true or false. To know the meaning of a proposition means to know how its truth-value is arrived at. This is because the meaning of a proposition is not different from the method of verification. There are two types of verification. Verification can be either "practically/empirically possible" or "logically possible", i.e. possible in principle.[4] In the case of logical possibility of verification, there will be no contradiction if I utter the statement "I discovered today what is occurring at the surface of the star". This is not self-contradictory but to discover it today is empirically impossible on the ground of certain scientific considerations.[5] Thus, it is logically but not empirically possible to verify the statement. In this regard, it is stated that what is empirically possible is also logically possible but not vice versa. The distinction between these two statements of verification is sometimes described as verifiability in practice and verifiability in theory. Many of the scientific generalizations are verifiable in theory. However, there are propositions which cannot be verified in either of senses. Metaphysical sentences are of this type. Bradley's sentence quoted by Ayer "The absolute enters into, but is itself incapable of, evolution and progress"[6] is neither verifiable in theory nor in practice.

Further, to logical positivists classified verification is of two types. They are:

1. Strong sense of verification.
2. Weak sense of verification.

In the case of "strong sense of verification", the truth of a proposition could be established conclusively in terms of our sense

---

[4] This is viewed by Ayer. See Ayer 1976: 48.

[5] This example is taken from Hospers 1967: 261.

[6] This sentence has been used in various places in the writings of logical positivists. It has been randomly taken from F.H. Bradley's *Appearance and Reality*, see Ayer 1976: 49.

experience whereas in the case of "weak sense of verification", verification can never be conclusively established. For example the statement "My computer is on the table". This can be verified through direct observation or perception, i.e. if one ventures into my room, he/she can see a computer on the table. Hence, the truth-value of the proposition is determined by the "strong sense of verifiability". But if I say "there is a *neem* tree nearer to my home". In this case, the hearer may not be able to find the exact and accurate home where I have been living. Though he may find a *neem* tree adjacent to somebody's house, he will be in doubt whether this house is the right one or not where I am living. Such a form of verification gets the status of the weak sense of verification. Here, the verification cannot be considered as a strong one. It is pointed out that though factual statements are verified conclusively, they can also be verified in weak sense of the term. Therefore, claim logical positivists, "verification" can be possible in two ways, direct and indirect.

From their viewpoint meaning of a proposition is itself a method of verification but "method of verification" is not a means to get the meaning of a proposition. For example:

1. I shall drive to my village.
2. I shall walk to my village.

Here, there are two ways for doing the same thing with respect to spatial distance. As far as the meaning of a proposition is concerned we can say that we will verify these two propositions to get their truth-value. This is because the method of the verification of a statement is not something that is added to the meaning of a proposition. A proposition already contains the method of its verification. So, we need not look for a method of verification. A proposition is verified means it must have meaning which implies a proposition does not possess truth-value until we verify its meaning, i.e. what it states about is precise. The meaning of a proposition reveals us under which circumstances the proposition will be regarded as true or false. Therefore, meaning is the criterion by which we can determine the truth-value of a proposition.

Is Conclusive Verification Possible?

If all the meaningful propositions are verified and the method of verification is the meaning of a proposition then the question arises, can we conclusively verify all the empirical statements? Further, what about the universal statements? Is it possible for us to verify the universal statements? Waismann argues that empirical statements are not completely or conclusively verified due to this nature which he calls "open texture". He enunciates that we cannot completely verify a proposition because there will be always something which remains to be verified. This will be clear from the following example. Let us consider a proposition, "There is a pen in the drawer of my table". Now the question arises, how to be certain about it? Is it sufficient for us if we go to the table and see that there is a pen in the drawer or, should we touch the object and feel its hardness or, should we check whether the object fulfils the purpose of writing? Let us assume that all these verifications are over. Even then Waismann argues we cannot be certain whether that particular object will be called a pen or not. In other words, we may still be in doubt whether the object which we have verified is to be called a pen or not. This happens because there may be cases where the object exactly looks like a pen but in reality it is something other than a pen. This incompleteness arises due to "open texture". Further, Waismann holds that the phrase "open texture" should not be confused with the term "vagueness". Vagueness can be removed by giving more accurate rules whereas open texture cannot be.

From the above analysis, it is understood that a factual statement or an empirical statement cannot be verified conclusively due the following reasons:

i. There are unlimited numbers of tests.

ii. Constituent words or terms of a statement involve open texture.

The first one states that we can never completely give the description of a material object or of a situation because there is a possibility that we may encounter with a new experience which we have never imagined before. The second one expresses our incomplete knowledge of the fact. Whatever way we describe a fact at no point of time we can claim that this is the final description of that fact. This happens because we even do not know what sorts of ascriptions are required for describing a fact. Further, there might be a possibility for a new discovery which would affect the whole interpretation of the earlier described fact.

In our everyday communication we understand the statements used by others without verification. Now the question arises, how is it possible that without verification we understand the meaning of the statements? Waismann answers

> We understand them (sentences) because we understand the single words which occur in them and grasp the grammatical structure of the sentence as a whole. The question of verification arises only when we come across a new sort of combination of words".[7]

For example, we understand the sentences like "The table is brown" and "The cow is an animal", because in those sentences all the words are familiar to us. So we do not need the criterion of verifiability to understand these sentences. But somebody utters a sentence "The cat thinks". Here we are perplexed to know the meaning of the statement, i.e. what the speaker really wants to say or means by uttering the sentence "The cat thinks". In this case just knowing the meaning of each constituent word of the sentence and its grammatical structure is not sufficient for us to understand the sentence. So, we have to describe the circumstances under which the statement will be regarded as true or false. In other words, we need to describe its method of verification. Thus, explaining the meaning of a proposition is to explain the method of verification

---

[7] Waismann 1951: 36.

under which the statement will be regarded as true or false. Hence, meaning and verification are closely connected with each other. The above discussion affirms that we understand the meaning of a proposition when we are able to describe the necessary conditions under which the statement will be judged as true.

The verifiability criterion does not demand that to know the meaning of a proposition is to know whether the proposition is true or false. But it demands that we must be able to describe theoretically a way in which the assertion could be examined; if not theoretically then we must be able to examine it in practice. This is because there are cases where we understand a proposition without knowing its truth-value. Thus, verifiability criterion itself is the meaning of a proposition. It helps to search out the truth-value of a proposition in order to claim whether a proposition is true or false. "The criterion of verifiability" and "the verifiability principle" are not the same though they appear to be same. The difference lies not in degree but in kind. The criterion of verifiability states whether a given statement has meaning or not, whereas the verifiability principle states "What does the meaning of a statement consist in or refer to?" Hence, the criterion of verifiability is a modest method to express that there is no meaning if there is no method of verification. In this connection, A.J. Ayer writes:

> We say that a sentence is factually significant to any person if and only if (s)he knows how to verify the proposition which it purports to express — that is, if (s)he knows what observation would lead him/her, under certain conditions, to accept the proposition as being true, or reject it as being false. — 1976: 48

So a common way of finding out what someone means or says by a statement is to ask how we might set about verifying it. If we cannot verify a proposition then the proposition is not only meaningless but also incoherent.

Still, the question remains, i.e. are the universal statements meaningful or not on the basis of the verifiability criterion? In other words, if we consider the verifiability criterion as a source of meaningfulness of a proposition then what will be the status of the universal statements?

Are the Universal Statements Meaningless?

The analysis of verifiability theory of meaning raises an important question: "Are the universal statements meaningless?" Logical positivists answer to this question by saying that universal statements do have meanings in the same way as the particular or individual statements have. But we have the deficiency for not being able to imagine the possible situations where we can verify the universal statement. This problem will be resolved if we consider the "weak sense of verifiability" as defined by A.J. Ayer in his *Language, Truth and Logic.* The truth of a proposition could be established by our experience but at the same time it is possible for our experience to render the truth of the statement probable. Holding this view, Carnap in his paper on "Testability and Meaning" says that "if we knew what it would be for a given sentence to be found true then we would know what its meaning is" (Ammerman 1965: 131).

Further, Carnap adds that to say a statement is verifiable or conclusively verifiable is to test the given statement through our empirical experience or observational sense-data. Thus, testability is the criterion for determining the meaning of a proposition. He used two expressions "material idiom" and "formal idiom"[8] as the criteria for determining the meanings of propositions. The first one states about the facts of the phenomenal world whereas the second one expresses about the events of remote past and of future. So both idioms contrast to each other in relation to their propositional attitude. The most important point here is that though they are distinct in virtue of their propositional attitude, all the formal idioms can be reduced to material idioms

[8] These two idioms are borrowed from Carnap's "Testability and Meaning" in Ammerman 1965: 137.

to determine their truth-value. They are reduced with the help of our observational sense-data statements. As a result, we are able to claim the truth-value of these two sorts of idioms which are represented in the form of propositions. Continuing his argument he explains that the difference between particular proposition and universal proposition is in degree but not in kind. This difference he points out on the basis of verifiability principle. For example, "All swans are white". This is a universal statement and it is true that we cannot verify all the swans in relation to the present, past and future time. So what we could do is that we will derive a few statements from the universal one, such as; *X* is white under certain specific conditions, *Y* is white under certain conditions, and let these two statements be verified through our experiences. From these verifications, we can assume that if and only if all swans come under the same conditions and considerations then all the swans will be white in colour. Here, we tempt to argue that when logical positivists stated about the verifiability theory, they presume two principles: (a) causal inferences, and (b) deductive argument.[9] Thus, the universal proposition "All swans are white" is meaningful and significant to us. Hence, we can draw the truth-value of the universal proposition "All swans are white" by claiming that under what conditions swans are white and under what conditions swans are not white. Considering a proposition about the past, for example, "John crossed the Alps". It is logically impossible now to verify whether John had done that job or not. This is because there is no such evidence. Neither John nor the person who witnessed John doing that act is available in the present society. So how could we derive the truth-value of this statement? Logical positivists answer that "John crossed the Alps" is a member of the general class of facts, "men crossing mountains". And we can observe the fact that "*X* is a man and he crossed the mountain". From this observational experience we can know the truth-value of the proposition "John crossed the Alps". Hence, the statement is significant for us. This

[9] These two principles are suggested by Stace 1947: 216.

sort of verification of statements, according to W.T. Stace, is called "the principle of observable kinds".[10] He defines this phrase as:

> A sentence, in order to be significant, must assert or deny facts which are of a kind or class such that it is logically possible directly to observe some facts which are instances of that class or kind. And if a sentence purports to assert or deny facts which are of a class or kind such that it would be logically impossible directly to observe any instance of that class or kind, then the sentence is non-significant. — Stace 1947: 218

On the above analysis, one may point out that if we consider the principle of observable kinds then there is a possibility to go into infinite regress. This is so because our verification at no point of time can ensure the certainty of the fact expressed by a proposition. In this regard, logical positivists argue that this notion matches with the empirical statement, i.e. we cannot be assured that our verification on an empirical statement is a complete one and at the same time we also cannot claim that there won't be any further verification after our verification is over. In this respect, A.J. Ayer states that all the factual statements may be considered as hypotheses in a very strict and logical sense.[11] Elaborating more on it he expresses that hypothesis means provisional supposition which sometimes assume as true and sometimes definitely confuted. So, we cannot hold the genuineness of a proposition. This is because it depends on the possibility of its definite confutation. There is no finite series of observations which is ever sufficient to establish the truth of a hypothesis beyond all possibilities of doubt. In this sense, all the factual statements are regarded as hypotheses.

Shifting their argument from factual assertions to ethical assertions, logical positivists claim that ethical assertions will be treated same as metaphysical assertions on the ground of not having their truth-value. Since they do not have truth-value, they

---

[10] Stace 1947: 218.

[11] This is expressed in different ways in various places in Ayer 1976.

will be considered as meaningless statements. So for them, ethical assertions must be removed from the corpus of the meaningful propositions of a language system.

Ethical Assertions and the Verifiability Criterion

Considering the issue of meaningfulness of ethical assertions, Carnap states that ethical assertions cannot be subjected to empirical investigation.[12] This is so because ethical assertions deal with the actions of human beings. They are the results of psychological and sociological considerations that give rise to the feelings, volitions, desires. So it is not a matter of investigating the fact rather it is to judge what is good in contrast to what is bad, what is evil, what is right, what we should do, etc. Succinctly speaking, the verifiability criterion does not apply to the ethical assertions, for they cannot be verified. It is obvious that the behaviour of an individual cannot be verified as is done in the case of factual statements. The behaviour of an individual is subject to changes whereas the fact of an assertion about the phenomenal world remains unchanged. Furthermore, the objectivity involves with the factual propositions when we verify the propositions but the same is not equivalently found in the case of ethical assertions. The reason is that all the ethical assertions deal with the notion of subjectivity. Since ethical assertions involve subjectivity their truth-value is indeterminable.

All the ethical statements are either in the form of requests or commands which do not satisfy the features to claim their truth-value whereas factual propositions are those which may be represented in the form of assertive or declarative kind, and that can be judged as either true or false. We cannot verify a proposition which is in the form of command or request but we can verify a proposition which describes something about the state of affairs of the world. In this regard, Carnap aptly expressed that all the ethical

[12] This phenomenon is analysed in Carnap 1981: 205.

statements mislead the grammatical form of factual assertions.[13] Hence, ethical assertions can neither be counted as true nor as false.

On the above account logical positivists claim that ethical statements do not have the factual contents. For example, "X has done wrong for not giving respect to his teacher". Here, if I say "X behaves wrongly", it is in no way affecting the sentence which I hold earlier. In this case I am simply evincing my moral disapproval to X. This is no way related to the factual content of a proposition; rather it deals with the feeling of mine (speaker). This elucidation expresses that there is no factual content found in ethical statements to be accounted for or judged as either true or false. This envisages that moral assertions are expressed all the way through moral sentiments. Somebody can disagree with my moral statements but cannot contradict with me. In this respect, A.J. Ayer states that ethical judgements are purely emotive. Ethical judgements are expressed feeling about certain objects, but not to make any assertion about them.[14] Thus ethical assertions could not be verified. So they are meaningless, according to logical positivists.

Further, logical positivists convey that ethical statements are not really statements at all because they are unable to judge as true or false on the ground of the verifiability criterion of meaning. In this regard, A.J. Ayer argues that when one considers how these ethical statements are actually used, it may be found that they function so very differently from other types of statements that it is advisable to put them into a separate category altogether. Yet after all, if someone still wishes to say that ethical statements are statements of fact, it is only a queer sort of fact, he is welcome to do so.[15] Putting emphasis on the term "queerness" of moral facts, it is confirmed that Ayer means to say that moral statements are not really of factual kind. They cannot come under the factual

---

[13] Carnap 1981: 206.

[14] This is expressed in Ayer 1976: 143.

[15] This is vividly explained in Ayer 1965: 231-33.

assertions. This is so because ethical assertions do not enhance the verifiability theory in order to determine their cognitive meaning and hence their truth-value is indeterminable.

From the above analysis, it is asserted that logical positivist's account on meaning can be treated as atomistic theory of meaning. The reason is that their basic aim is to establish the meaning of a proposition through the verifiability method. Hence, they propose the theory called "verifiability theory" which evinces that to determine the meaning of a proposition is to determine the criterion of verifiability under which the proposition will be judged as true or false. So for them, the sense of a proposition is the method of its verification.[16]

As we have stated in our earlier presentations meaning of atomism deals only with individual sentences and each sentence conveys its meaning without corroborating other sentences. This is what is exactly propounded by the logical positivists when they advocate the "verifiability theory of meaning". They argue that meaning of a proposition deals with the facts or states of affairs of the world and the verifiability criterion will help us to decide whether the proposed fact correctly maps with the facts of the world or not. If it correctly maps then the proposition will be treated as true and if it does not correctly map then the proposition is treated as false. Hence, truth-value of a proposition is determined through its verifiability method.

---

[16] This is enounced by Schlick and Waismann in conversation with Wittgenstein while discussing the issue on the determination of the meaning of a proposition in a language. See Munitz 1981: 228.

5

The Untenability of Atomistic Theory of Meaning

IN THE earlier chapters, we have discussed the primal concern of atomistic theory of meaning with reference to individual sentence. We argued that atomistic theory of meaning or "meaning atomism" expresses that a representation either in linguistic or mental system is completely definable by itself. It explains, meaning of a sentence is determined in isolation from other sentences of a language, which implies understanding a proposition does not require any support from other propositions of that language, and this theory is endorsed by Frege, early Wittgenstein, Schlick, Ayer, Waismann, Alfred Tarski and a few. For them, each sentence conveys a specific sense and it is about the state of affairs of the world. The sentence will be meaningful if the state of affairs is found in the phenomenal world, and thereby, the sentence is judged as true. So there is a tight-knit association found between meaning of a proposition and its referred state of affairs. Thus, a proposition is judged as true or false is based on its referred state of affairs. If the state of affairs conveyed by the sentence maps with the empirical world then the sentence will be judged as true, and it will be judged as false if the state of affairs does not map with the empirical world. The important idea derived from this conception of meaning is that the truth-value of a proposition determines the meaning of a proposition. Logically speaking, if a proposition does not have truth-value, it will be regarded as meaningless proposition.

A series of questions arise from the above discussions, such as; "can meaning of an individual sentence be understood without relating to other sentences?"; "how the meaning of an individual sentence will be understood independently from other sentences?"; "how does a sentence convey a particular sense, and again, eternally that must about the state of affairs of the world?"; "how does sense assist to get the referent of it?" All these questions together constitute a broad query of our discussion in this paper, i.e. what are the problems found in atomistic theory of meaning to claim its inadequacies to capture the whole complexity of meaning? Let us discuss the logical grounds on the failure of atomistic theory of meaning in any language system.

Logical positivists, such as Ayer, Schlick and Waismann, in confirmation to the theory of "meaning atomism", state that the meaning of a proposition is the method of its verification. From this, it follows that a sentence is verifiable when it implies that it possesses a certain meaning, and the "meaning" is derived from the observational sense-data[1] or the sense experiences. In this regard, Carl Hempel states that "'verifiability criterion' cannot be considered as a sole criterion to understand the meaning of a proposition".[2] The reasons he has mentioned that there are cases where propositions are in universal form or in the form of scientific laws. These propositions are neither verified conclusively nor able to provide the complete observational sense-data to establish their truth-values, but they possess meaning. So, in this case, how could we claim that these propositions are meaningless? Continuing further he enunciates that there are statements that are emotive in form or expressing moral aspirations of individuals whose cognitive value cannot be determined by verifiability method. Then, could we regard these as a "pseudo-hypothesis"? How should we consider these statements? Can we claim that they are necessarily meaningless propositions? Thus, the verifiability criterion for determining the meaning of a proposition is enunciated with

---

[1] The phrase "Observational Sense-data" has introduced by Bertrand Russell in his paper "Descriptions". See, Russell 1965: 15-24.

[2] Hempel: 1935.

some serious lacunas. It is so because it fails to explain a proper account of meaning determination of a proposition, particularly, the complexities associated with it.

A question arises, whether the verifiability criterion for determining the meaning of a proposition is a private one or of a public sort? This question has utmost significance in this situation because in order to verify a proposition there are varieties of method available to us. In other words, there is no single method that has been prescribed to do so. We verify a proposition by the help of our sense experiences and the evidences that are accessible to us. Thus, it is claimed that the method of verifying a proposition may differ from person to person and from place to place. If it is so then how could we determine the meaning a proposition with certainty?

In view of the logical positivists' rigid distinctions between the analytic and synthetic propositions, it is necessary to consider the case like, where the proposition is neither analytic nor synthetic but possesses meaning, e.g. "I request him to open the door". This sentence is neither analytic, that is, true by definition, nor it is synthetic because it does not state any facts of the world. None the less, it possesses meaning. So a question arises, where do we place this sentence and how to determine the logical status of it? Hence, the principle of verification cannot be applied for the determination of the meanings of such sentences.

The verifiability criterion cannot even apply to those statements which are consisting of both universal and existential quantifiers in order to acquire their meaning. For example: "For any substance there exists some solvent".[3] This sentence consists of both universal and particular quantifiers.[4] The question arises that what sort of observations lead to verify the facts stand by

[3] This example was taken from Hempel 1965: 218.

[4] Here "particular quantifier" is to be understood same as "existential quantifier". The symbol for existential quantifier is $\exists x$.

these propositions? It is noticed that no sentences of this kind can be logically deduced from any finite set of observation sentences. Hence, it is unverifiable and thus the sentence is not meaningful. But in reality, we understand the proposition and we also know what it expresses by virtue of its meaning. In this respect, the criterion of verifiability is found to be too defective.

Logically speaking, if there are two sentences, "The table is brown — *T*" and "The absolute is perfect — *N*" and they are conjoined with disjunctive operators where, if one is verifiable the whole sentence will be also verifiable. Symbolically speaking, if *T* and *N* are two different sentences where both are conjoined in terms of disjunctive operator (*T* v *N*) where if one, such as *T* is verifiable the entire sentence *T* v *N* is verifiable. The reason is, if *T* is a consequence of some finite class of observation sentences then trivially (*T* v *N*) is a consequence of the same class. This sort of case logical positivists have not taken into their account for establishing the verifiability theory of meaning. Verifiability theory claims a sentence *P* is verifiable, and hence it has meaning, and the meaning of the sentence is derived from observational sense-data.[5] Considering this phenomenon, it follows that ~*P* (negation of *P*) cannot be verified because it is logically deduced from the rule that if *P* is true then *P* must be false, and if *P* is true then *P* is false. If we add the quantifiers with the proposition *P* we find that "if '$\exists x$ (*Px*)" is true then its negation "$\forall x$ (~*Px*)" is false and vice versa. Since the existential quantifier says that there exists at least one thing that has the property *P*, whereas, the second one or the universal quantifier says, nothing has the property *P*. A question arises, if we verify the proposition $\exists x$ (*Px*) and get its meaning, we can claim that $\exists x$ (*Px*) is true but why can't we claim that $\forall x$ (~*Px*) is also true. Why can't we say that $\forall x$ (~*Px*) also possesses meaning, therefore, it must be true? If we say so, then it will be a logical error to claim that both *P* and its negation ~*P* are true. In this respect the atomistic theory of meaning is too inclusive.

---

[5] The phrase "observational sense-data" has introduced by Russell 1965: 15-24. Also see Russell 1993.

Further, in case of atomistic theory of meaning we do not get the meanings of the sentences that are expressed in the forms of existential hypotheses. For example, "There exists at least one dragon". It is a proposition where we are unable to explain the meaning independently from other propositions because, in order to know the meaning of this sentence, we must know what the dragon is about. It is through this process that we will know the meaning of the given proposition. Thus, the meaning of a proposition can be attained only when we know in which context it is used and what it states about. Suppose the sentence *P* says "All crows are black" and *Q* says "The absolute is perfect". *P* is verifiable as an atomic sentence. We get its meaning by the help of the criterion of verifiability theory because it states about the facts of the world. On the other hand, *Q* does not state anything about the facts of the world. Hence, it is unverifiable, but we get its meaning by the help of its constituent words and by using the grammatical rules on it. Thus, it is asserted that *P* is true and *Q* is false on account of the verifiability theory of meaning. Logically speaking, if *Q* is false then $Q \wedge P$ (two sentences are conjoined with the logical connectives, symbolized as "and") must be false. This is so because in case of disjunction out of two premises if one is false the conclusion will be also false, i.e. "All crows are black and the absolute is perfect" is false by virtue of the falsity of later proposition. But this is wrong to say that "All crows are black and the absolute is perfect" is a false sentence. Here, atomistic theory fails to determine the meaning of a proposition.

Let us consider another case where *T* is a sentence and it is empirically significant for satisfying the verifiability criterion of meaning. The question arises; if *T* is a significant observable sentence then $\sim T$ is not an observable significant sentence. So $\sim T$ does not have the cognitive meaning as opposed to *T*. But it is logically wrong to say so. Here, atomistic theory fails to establish the meaning of a proposition on the ground of verifiability criterion of meaning.

Carnap's expresses his views on "meaning atomism" in his work on *The Logical Syntax of Language* (1937)[6] and that is purely based on the mathematical logic and empirical sciences. According to him,

> . . . the matter of "verification" is still to be approached in a syntactical way; that is, as a matter of the formal, syntactical coherence or consistency within the language of an empirical discipline, among the various propositions that compose it. So, any empirical science will need to include in its language the protocol sentences that report the findings of empirical observations. — Munitz 1981: 266[7]

This view can be questioned on the ground that we cannot claim that the formal or syntactical rules are essential for doing the logical analysis of the language of science. If we do so, then it ignores the crucial semantic part of the empirical reference and it leads to the determination of the truth-value of a proposition.

It is useful to say, the meaning of a statement is the method of its verification. But to say this is not to make a claim that we can determine the meaning of a proposition once for all. This is the case because in our day-to-day life, we don't think of verification when we understand the meaning of the propositions uttered by the speakers. We suggest a method of verification only after we understand the meaning of a proposition. This may be argued in the following way. If a person knows what it means that "it is now raining" and also knows the word "yesterday" means, then he understands the sentence "it rained yesterday". It is so because he understands the constituent words of the sentence and knows the usage of English syntax. This, however, does not mean that I know how the proposition is to be verified. Then if that is the case, what is it that leads me to suggest a particular method of verification? I have learned from experience that rain leaves traces of moisture on the earth. I remember such experiences and say that on the

---

[6] Carnap 1937.

[7] Munitz 1981: 266.

basis of this evidence it can be determined whether it has rained yesterday or not.[8] This case clearly shows that to explain the method of verification is not to explain the meaning.

Let us consider another example: "This man died five hours ago".[9] This sentence has meaning and we understand it without verifying the proposition. The explanation is as follows; if I am asked whether I have understood this sentence, I would say that I do; otherwise I cannot claim that I know English. But if I am asked how do I verify the sentence, I may not be in a position what to say. Suppose it is discovered that the exact death time of the person by conducting certain medical tests. Still, I would not say "Ah! now at last I understand what the sentence means". The reason is that the meaning of the sentence had already been established before that discovery.

Wittgenstein while speaking about verification principle says that it is "a mere rule of thumb", because "verification" may not imply expressing meaning. As he argues, statements in the newspaper can verify the proposition that Cambridge had won the boat race, and that yet these statements "only go a very little way towards explaining the meaning of 'boat race'".[10] Thus, the verifiability theory of meaning which is a part of atomistic theory of meaning fails to be a proper theory of meaning because of its failure to see that an expression or a sentence can be meaningful on various considerations and not on the consideration of verifiability criterion alone. In this respect, we should further point out that most of the difficulties arise in connection with verifiability theory are due to the atomistic conception of meaning that it assumes in its foundation. Its approach to language is erroneous.

Language is not a collection of isolated individual sentences.

---

[8] This example and its analysis are taken from Waismann 1981: 52.

[9] Ibid.

[10] Moore 1959: 266. I have substituted "proposition" for "hypothesis" in this passage. See Hanfling 1981b: 25.

Sentences, on the other hand, form a conglomerate body where they are interlinked with each other. This brings a radical change in our conception of meaning. Since sentences are interconnected, the meaning of a sentence is decided not individually but holistically, i.e. by the network of sentences involved in the semantic relationship. In view of this semantic holism the criterion of verifiability no longer looks promising. The reason is the verification of a sentence cannot be restricted to the sentence alone. Because, to verify a sentence means to verify many other sentences which are connected to it. This inevitably follows from the holistic nature of meaning which subsequently shows how inadequate the positivists' criterion of verifiability and the notion of meaning that it seeks to support it.

We will now examine Frege's notion of "meaning atomism" with a view to show why it fails as a theory to give an adequate account of meaning. The basic problems for Frege is: first, to explain how propositions get their meanings; second, how the truth-values of these propositions are determined.

Drawbacks of Frege's Meaning Atomism

According to Frege, sense is logically prior to reference. The sense of a proposition is the same as the thought of a proposition, which for him, is the meaning of a proposition. Each proposition expresses a sense that is about the state of affairs of the world. And, if that state of affairs maps with the phenomenal world then the proposition is judged as true, and if it does not map, the proposition is judged as false. Thus, for him, the referent of a proposition is same as truth-value of the proposition. He enunciates that truth-value of a proposition is a composite substratum made up of concepts and objects. But he does not hold this doctrine for long due to the difficulties that arise in connection with the determining of references of propositions; for example, the statement "The capital of India". Here, the reference of the complex expression "the capital of India" is composed of "the capital of ( )" and "India". We thus find that there are two references "New Delhi" and "India", and both of them are to be satisfied to get the truth-value of the proposition. Now the question arises, which one among these two should refer to "India" or "New Delhi". In other words, how do we get the truth-value of the proposition "The capital of India" whether by referring to India or by referring to New Delhi? This gives rise to a dilemma – a dilemma regarding referring to the exact object. Thus, the "meaning atomism" is not a satisfactory theory to determine whether a proposition is true or false.

Furthermore, the problem arises due to the failure of determining the sense of a proposition. In the atomistic theory of meaning, we often find propositions with having proper names. We get the meaning of a proper name through definite descriptions. So, the meaning of all proper names can be accounted through their definite descriptions. As Frege says, every definite description has sense and from sense we can determine the referent of it. The problem subsists when we have a proper name with having more than one description, where all the descriptions are true of the proper name. For example, the proper name "Aristotle" can be described as, "The author of the *Nicomachean Ethics*", "The disciple of Plato", "The teacher of Alexander the Great", etc. here, could we say that each description is equivalent with other descriptions on the basis of the sense criterion? If our answer is affirmative then we make a mistake because the sense of the description "The teacher of Alexander the Great" becomes the same as sense of the description "The author of the *Nicomachean Ethics*". But this will mean that all these propositions are analytic, which necessarily implies the meaning of "Aristotle" becomes equivalent with descriptions used for Aristotle. But this is incorrect since the meaning of "Aristotle" is not same as its descriptions.

In Frege's account of meaning it is found that the sense of a proposition is described as the "mode of presentation".[11] Here, a question arises; if the sense of an expression is the mode of

[11] Frege 1948. Also see Currie 1980: 247.

presentation of its referent then it is impossible for a proper name to have the same sense because of the variations found in the descriptions associated with it. Each description will present their referent in quite different ways. Thus it is stated that "a name is not true of its bearer, not as a description arbitrarily correlated with an object".[12] On these grounds, atomistic theory of meaning as expressed through Frege's theory fails to give a logically coherent account of meaning.

Atomistic theory of meaning forms the basis of the referential theory of meaning. It is so because the referential theory of meaning follows the same procedures as meaning atomism does to understand the meaning of a proposition. It states that meaning of an expression is to be understood in relation to its corresponding objects/referents. But this theory does not hold the "meaning atomism" as free from logical problems.

Problems with the Referential Theory of Meaning

Referential theory of meaning is restricted to only assertive sentence. Its scope is not so widened to incorporate other varieties of sentences those we use in our day-to-day life for communication purposes. We do not only use those sentences but also understand them and identify their referents. In relation to the identification of the referent of an assertive proposition, referential theory of meaning claims that there is a mapping found between the sense of a proposition and the facts of the world. This forces us to claim that meaning is same as its referent. But the usage of ordinary language does not confirm to this conception. For example, "Tranz is brown". If a speaker utters this sentence without mentioning the context, the hearer is invariably assumed "Tranz" is a proper name. But, the proper name Tranz does not refer to any object. So, how could we understand the meaning of the proposition? Again, if the meaning of an expression is just its referent then we would expect that any two expressions having the same referent could

[12] Bell 1979: 56.

be substituted with one for the other for their meaning. If we do so, then we will be faced with insuperable difficulties explained in the following example:

1. Tom wants to meet the supreme commander of the Indian armed forces.
2. Tom wants to meet the President of India.

Here, these two expressions have different meanings but they refer to one person. Now a question arises, could we substitute one for the other as they have same referent? We cannot do so, otherwise, these two sentences will be treated as analytic, which is logically incorrect/wrong. Analytic sentences are judged as necessarily true sentences by virtue of their definition. We do not require any experience (verification) to claim about their truth. It is so because the predicate invariably repeats in the subject. But these two sentences are not analytic in their structure. To understand the meaning of these two sentences we need to verify the facts that the sentences are stating about. As a result, unlike two analytic sentences which refer to one referent, we can neither synonymously nor interchangeably use one with the other. If we do so then we will mislead the meaning of the sentences which is logically wrong in the usage of language. Further, there is no basis on which we can say that the two propositions laid above are identical. Thus, referential theory of meaning, which is a form of atomistic theory of meaning, does not stay away with lacunas for determining the meanings of propositions.

The presence of atomistic theory of meaning is also found in the Wittgensteinean picture theory of meaning[13] where it expresses that each proposition is a picture of a particular state of affairs of the world. The proposition will be true if the picture corresponds to the facts of the world, and if it does not, then it is judged as false. But this view is rejected on some logical grounds elucidated in the following passages.

[13] Wittgenstein 1972: Sect. 4.021.

Picture Theory of Meaning and Its Inadequacy

Picture theory of meaning is a version of the atomistic theory of meaning which reflects from the explanations that a sentence is meaningful when it corresponds with the fact existing in the world. A sentence is thus meaningful by virtue of its correspondence with the external reality. The picture, that a sentence depicts, is the sense or the essence of that sentence. Generally, it is understood as the meaning of a sentence.

A question arises here, i.e. is the world divided into facts or things? Wittgenstein in his *Tractatus* says that the world is the totality of facts but not of things.[14] But in his later work *Philosophical Investigations*, he revised this idea. As he explains, every fact constitutes with different objects in a determinate way. When we observe a fact we do not know about its exact nature. We come to know it through its constituent parts and the way they are combined into a whole. For example, "a chess-board, we are probably thinking of the composition out of thirty-two white and thirty-two black squares, but could we not also say, for instance, that it was composed of the colours black and white and the schema of squares".[15] In reality, we find that facts are necessarily associated with different things or objects. So it is the aggregation of things that makes a fact. Thus, constructing a fact is a subjective concept. Since it is subjective, it differs from person to person. So, the fact that a sentence represents is not of objective kind. The idea of correspondence may thus go wrong. This trembles the ground of the picture theory of meaning which claims that the picture of a sentence corresponds to the facts of the world by virtue of which we understand the proposition.

A logical objection can be made against the picture theory of meaning in particular and the atomistic theory of meaning in general. That is, the picture theory of meaning deals with assertive

---

[14] Wittgenstein 1972: Sect. 1.1.

[15] Ibid. 2001: Sect. 47.

sentences whose truth-value can be determined. So there will be no problem for us to form a picture of those sentences. Now the question arises regarding the negative propositions, i.e. "how can we form a picture of a negative proposition?" Take the proposition, "Cows are not dogs". In this case the correspondence theory fails to determine the truth-value of the proposition. It is so because if we analyse the proposition through classical logic, this proposition would fail to convey the meaning of what "cows" are, simply because it negates a single possibility of how we understand the word "cow", which, in this case, would leave the idea of a "cow" open to a lot of different predicates, such as "A cow is anything except a dog". Even in this situation, the proposition does not convey a legitimate meaning because of the referent problems involved with the expression "anything". Thus, we are not getting the exact referent what the sentence is stating about. Further, there are no such circumstances where we can form the picture of the state of affairs expressed by the proposition. Thus we are unable to refer to the fact that the proposition is stating about. Hence, on the account of picture theory of meaning it is a meaningless proposition. But could we claim so? If the answer is "yes" then it indicates that there is something essentially wrong with the picture theory of meaning.

Further, in atomistic theory of meaning we find that every proposition has a definite sense. Since it provides the definite and determinate senses that correspond to the facts of the world. Thus, each proposition is meaningful based on its corresponding facts that exist in the phenomenal world. But this does not offer a theory of meaning that can account for all sorts of propositions in our language.

> For example, suppose someone says "leave this or that open". Here, the sentence nevertheless provides a definite sense. Rather, it holds the indefinite sense that would really not be a sense at all. — This is like: "An indefinite boundary is not really a boundary at all". Here, one thinks perhaps: if I say "I have locked up the

> man in the first room — there is only one door left open" — then I simply have not locked him at all; his being locked in is a shame. One would be inclined to say here: you have not done anything at all. An enclosure with a hole in it is as good as none — but is that true? — *Philosophical Investigations*, Sect. 99[16]

To hold the criterion of meaningfulness of a proposition, picture theory of meaning states that it is the elementary proposition which states about the facts of the world. We determine the truth-value of an elementary proposition on the basis of its correspondence to the worldly affairs. A question pops up, i.e. is it necessary that all the propositions should be reducible to elementary propositions? Furthermore, do we communicate with others only through elementary propositions? Obviously not, yet we understand the meaning of the propositions without deducing them to elementary propositions. In this sense, atomistic theory of meaning fails as a theory to explain how we understand the meaning of a proposition.

In atomistic theory of meaning we often find that propositions are consisting of proper names. The meaning of a proper name is determined by the object it denotes. This view is criticized in the *Philosophical Investigations.* As Wittgenstein argues, this view is the result of a confusion between the bearers of a name with the meaning of a name. For example, to say, "Plato dies" implies that the bearer of the name dies but not the meaning of the name dies. "It is a matter of fact that a man's name does not lose its meaning when he is destroyed."[17] The meaning of a name consists of various descriptions which are used for identifying the person which bears that name. But a name can have a meaning even though nothing exists corresponding to it, e.g. dragon. In this connection, Wittgenstein admits that there may be cases where we have to say "the word '———' would have no meaning if a certain object 0 did

[16] Wittgenstein 2001: Sect. 99.

[17] Ibid.: Sect. 55.

not exist."[18] But in these cases, the object 0 is not anything named by the word in question, and our statement is in fact a mere truism.

In picture theory of meaning, it is viewed that elementary propositions are the pictures of reality and they state the facts about the world. So, there is a "logical form" found between the picture of a proposition and the facts of the world. This analysis does not work in all the cases of ordinary language. For example, consider a case where a person made a gesture, familiar to Neopolitans as meaning something like disgust or contempt, and then he asks what is the logical form of that. To look for a logical form in a remote possibility, the view is that, a proposition is a picture of reality, i.e. what it describes is untenable.

Another difficulty is prominently figured in the atomistic theory of meaning, i.e. in reference to the relation between the word and the object it denotes or a sentence and the situation it describes. The question frames as, how is it possible to make a correlation between the language and the world? According to the atomists, it is possible by virtue of performing a mental act, namely intending that we can make a relation between the word and the object. This resulted into confusion with regard to correctly identifying the object. For example, *X* said to *Y* "Tom visited yesterday". What is it that *Y* understands from this sentence? Is it "Tom Rant" or "Tom Hick" who visited yesterday? In order to confirm this, *Y* asks further, who is that person visited yesterday – is it Tom Rant or Tom Hick? This example clearly shows that "mental act of intending" does not work in all the cases for understanding the meaning of a proposition. Hence, atomistic theory of meaning is too rigid and too narrow to give an indubitable account for the semantic behaviour of ordinary language.

One may point out that atomistic theory of meaning can function well with the support from ostensive definition where the truth-value of each proposition is determined ostensively. But the

---

[18] Pitcher 1972: 182.

method of ostensive definition has a very limited scope. It may fail to explain the meaning of all segments of language use. For example, a teacher says to a student, "This is blue by pointing out the finger to a blue pen". In this case, the student might think that the term "blue pen" is a name, or it may be the term "blue" which will occur when "blue pen" comes to his preview. Moreover, for that student "blue pen" is the blue color.[19] This shows that the very premise of the atomistic theory that the criterion of meaningfulness of a sentence is decided by its truth condition is untenable.

This theory claims, meaning of a sentence depends upon the meaning of its constituent words of that sentence. But this has failed on a logical ground. Take an example of "The father of Annette".[20] Here a question arises, how does the meaning of this expression depend on the meaning of its constituent part? In this sentence, the singular term "Annette" refers to Annette, while the complex term "the father of" is designated as *t* in the form of a singular term. Hence, it refers to the father of that person, to whom *t* refers. As a result, we are able to understand the meaning of this sentence and do communicate in our language. But if we know the meaning of each and every word of the sentence like, "the", "of", "father" and "Annette" and try to get the meaning out of it, we are not able to get the proper meaning of the sentence. So, we need a holistic view to understand this sentence, i.e. "each constituent word of the sentence must have the ontologically neutral sense of making the systematic contribution to the meaning of the sentence in which they occur".[21] In this sense meaning works holistically.

Finally, there is an important issue to be addressed concerning to the relationship between the Tarskian model of "T-schema" and the atomistic theory of meaning. The question here is how far the

---

[19] This analysis is found in an elaborate fashion in Schlick 1979: 458. See Parkinson 1988: 35.

[20] This example and its analysis are taken from Davidson 1984: 17-18.

[21] Ibid.: 22.

Tarskian model is successful in defending the atomistic theory of meaning.

Tarski and the Problem of "T-Schema"

Tarski is one of the supporters of atomistic theory of meaning. His schema "Convention-*T*" provides a well-formed definition of the truth theory which satisfies the atomistic theory of meaning. The definition that he offers claims that the two following principles must be satisfied for an individual sentence to be judged as true. First of all, it should be "formally correct" and second, it must be "materially adequate". His "*T*-Schema" is:

(*T*) *S* is true if and only if *P*.

Here *S* is the name of a sentence which can be judged as either true or false. *P* is the actual sentence which states about the facts or state of affairs of the world. In short, his definition states that *S* is true if and only if it is about the fact which is found in the empirical world. For example, "'snow is white' is true if and only if snow is white". The truth-value of the sentence "snow is white" depends on "snow" and the property of being "white". The sentence will be judged as true, only when all these things are verified by our observational sense data, otherwise the sentence is false.

The problem arises when we are asked, "how are we to tell whether a particular *T*-sentence is itself true". It is followed by a subsequent question, "how do we know what the meaning of an expression is about"? Again, it is argued that "how the intentional mental states or intentional sentences refer to things/objects"? Such as, "He is in bad mood". Some other sentences like, "Punctuality is praiseworthy", "Honesty is desirable", "Every particle of snow above a certain size is white", etc. These propositions have no particular references yet we understand these propositions. How is it possible to understand these propositions? In this regard, Putnam states that Tarski's truth predicates have nothing to do with semantics or the common conception of truth. In his words, "as a philosophical account of truth, Tarski's theory fails as badly as it is possible for an account to fail" (Davidson 1990: 285).[22] While criticizing Taski's truth theory, Max Black and Dummett are of the opinion that

> Tarski did not define the concept of truth, even as applied to sentences. What he showed is how to define a truth predicate for each of a number of well-behaved languages. — Ibid.[23]

Repudiating Tarski's truth theory, Kripke said that any one who knows how the bival condition operates in English must know that the sentence concerned expresses a truth irrespective of whether he knows the meaning of that sentence. For example, the sentence "Horses are called horses" is true without knowing the meaning of the proposition expressed by that sentence. It is an uninformative sentence. So we are not getting any new information from it. It only expresses analytic truth that is true by definition.

Counteracting to Tarski's truth theory it may be stated that it is neither possible to understand the meaning of a sentence by the help of its constituent words nor the sentence is itself capable of acquiring the meaning without corroborating with other sentences. Thus, we need a holistic view for understanding the meaning of a sentence which implies a sentence won't confirm our experiences exclusively or completely independent of other sentences of a language. For example, the sentence "The sun is behind the cloud"[24] is true if all the following conditions are satisfied, such as:

1. It is daytime.
2. The sun has risen.
3. It is not pitch dark.
4. More people are awake than asleep.
5. Millions of automobiles are emitting smoke in to the atmosphere, and so on.

---

[22] Davidson 1990: 285.

[23] Ibid.

[24] This example is borrowed from Wiggins 1997: 5-6.

This example shows a sentence won't be understood in isolation from other sentences.

From these above analyses, we assert that atomistic theory of meaning by nature is too narrow. It does not capture the complexities of meaning. So we need to look for an alternative conception of meaning, i.e. holistic approach to meaning. It submits that in order to understand the meaning of a sentence we need to understand some other sentences within a particular paradigm of language. This suggests for the holistic view of meaning, i.e. meaning works holistically.

6

Quine and Meaning Holism

QUINE IN the contemporary philosophy of language is widely known for breaking the age of old semantic tradition characterized by the atomistic approach to language and meaning. He develops an alternative approach or a model in semantics which shows how meaning works holistically. To establish this, he offers arguments which are cogent, systematic and exhaustive. Quine's idea of meaning holism thus assumes a rigorous theoretical basis. The objective of this chapter is to give a systematic representation of his theoretical basis in order to arrive at Quine's conception of meaning holism.

The theoretical basis of Quine's meaning holism consists of three major arguments. They are: his refutation of analytic-synthetic distinction, his exegesis of verifiability theory of meaning and the idea of interanimation of sentences which Quine talks about while explaining the process of learning language by us. These three arguments together form Quine's theory of meaning holism.

The aim of the first argument, namely the rejection of analytic-synthetic distinction is to prepare the ground for meaning holism to be considered as a viable option for explaining the semantic behaviour of language. The presence of analytic-synthetic distinction creates an obstacle to meaning holism because the notion of analyticity claims that there are sentences that are true by virtue of meanings and thus they are necessary and a priori. This way the analytic sentences confirm to atomistic theory of meaning because the meaning ascribed to these sentences is decided individually, i.e. independently of any other sentences.

The second argument concerns with Quine's critique of verifiability theory of meaning. In Quine's objection the fallacy of logical positivists is that sentences cannot be verified individually because sentences are related to other sentences and thereby they form a corporate body of sentences. Thus, the semantic thrust of verifiability theory is wrong. The third argument is Quine's idea of inter-animation of sentences which he develops along with his indeterminacy of translation.

We shall discuss Quine's meaning holism mainly in the light of these three interrelated arguments. Quine's argument for meaning holism can be found in various places of his work. But among these his essay on *Two Dogmas of Empiricism* and his *Word and Object* are the most important for our present discussion. In our deliberation, we will mainly focus on these works.

Quine's thesis on meaning holism cannot be presented as a linguistic thesis only, because it also has an epistemological thrust. While formulating meaning holism he considers logical positivists as his target of attack. This is evident from his first two arguments, namely, rejection of analytic–synthetic distinction and the critique of verificationist theory of meaning. The epistemic import of analytic–synthetic distinction is that it supports an epistemological perspective, namely, foundationalism which positivists advocate as the part of their theory of knowledge. Similarly, verificationist theory of meaning defends a particular form of relationship regarding how a theory is related to the world. In epistemic terms this leads to reductionism. Quine's third argument on meaning holism is presented along with his thesis on indeterminacy of translation. Indeterminacy of translation is an extension of his critique of verificationist theory of meaning which has the same epistemological bearing. In our approach to Quine's meaning holism we thus consider it not as a bare semantic thesis but project it as a semantic thesis with an epistemological underpinning. In Quine, the connection between meaning holism and epistemology follows from the connection between language and epistemology. This is particularly true in view of Quine's critique of the positivist theory of language and the theory of knowledge that is directly linked with it. With these introductory remarks concerning the thrust of our discussion to be undertaken in this presentation we will now go into the crux of our discussion.

The Linguistic and the Epistemological Basis of the Analytic–Synthetic Distinction

Logical positivism assumes an intimate connection between language and epistemology. This is clearly reflected in its stand on epistemology which is largely shaped and structured by its theory of language. The discussion of the latter is thus crucial to the understanding of the former. To do this we will be exploring the language–epistemology nexus of the positivism.

It is a well-known thesis of the positivists that scientific knowledge consists of two parts. The first part is empirical knowledge and the second part is mathematical and theoretical knowledge. Accordingly, the epistemological status of the respective parts is grounded on different conceptions. The former may be said to be grounded in traditional empiricist theory whereas the epistemological status of the latter is explained by the positivists by their notion of analyticity. It is a notion which in many respects is similar to that of Kant's notion of a priori. However, there is one fundamental difference which sharply distinguishes positivists' notion of analyticity from Kant's notion of a prioricity. Analytic statements for positivists do not say anything about the real world and in this sense they are contentless. It is this contentless nature of analytic statements that distinguishes them from synthetic a priori statements of Kant. Also it is important to note that being contentless these statements are immune to experience. As a result, they can never be criticized on the ground of any empirical consideration. They do not make any claim about the empirical world. It is due to this reason, analytic statements are treated separately having a privileged epistemological status with scientific theories. For positivists, the notion of analyticity which is coextensive with contentlessness is thus epistemologically analogous to what is traditionally conceived as a priori.

Positivists derive their notion of analyticity from their theory of language and meaning. Analytic statements are defined as true on the ground that they are true by virtue of their meaning alone. But how do the positivists arrive at this notion? This is where we come to the notion of language or linguistic framework which allows the notion of analyticity to be derived as part of its logical compulsion. Language is indispensable to talk about the world. But to do this we need to choose a language which in actual terms implies selecting a certain linguistic framework, i.e. grammar. Grammar is a system consisting of a set of syntactic and semantic interpretation rules. If a sentence is true by virtue of these syntactic and semantic rules, then the sentence is analytic. Since the truth of such sentences is determined by the framework itself, they are true independently of what the world is. In this sense, as we have said earlier, analytic sentences are contentless. Their contentlessness follows from two considerations. First, they owe their existence to linguistic framework alone. Second, the choice of linguistic framework itself is not based on any cognitive consideration. The considerations that play a major role in deciding a linguistic framework are pragmatic. How efficient a particular language is from some scientific purpose, for example, becomes important in choosing a linguistic framework. The question of truth does not figure prominently at all in this exercise. This is where we see that there is a sharp contrast between a linguistic framework and a theory. The choice of a theory is guided by truth or the actual–cognitive consideration whereas the choice of a linguistic framework is guided by the notion of efficiency.

This brings a clear division between pragmatic, on the one side, and cognitive on the other. Within these two broad divisions, analytic claims and factual or synthetic claims are situated. These are two primary modes through which respective claims are grounded. The one is grounded in the linguistic framework and other is grounded in the world. As a result, the two claims acquire two different epistemological statuses. In the former case, since the choice of linguistic framework is non-cognitive, the claims grounded in such a framework cannot be other than being cognitively contentless. This explains the non-refutable character of these claims by experience. High-level scientific and mathematical claims belong to this category. In contrast to this are the claims belonging to the latter category being grounded in the world of facts and experience. Their epistemological status is thus defined in the light of empirical and not pragmatic considerations. The distinction between the pragmatic and the cognitive corresponds to Carnap's[1] distinction between external and internal questions. The former involve choice of linguistic framework whereas the latter are concerned with the things that are falling within a physical framework. These internal questions are therefore "empirical scientific" questions which make true or false assertions about the world.

The above discussion shows that language–epistemology nexus of positivism gives rise to a particular form of foundationalism. Classification of sentences into analytic understood as contentless and synthetic understood as factual implies that they have different epistemological status. "Analytic" and "synthetic" are the two fundamental notions which provide the foundation for a theory of knowledge. It is a theory in which epistemology is seen as logical reconstruction of scientific theories. Against the backdrop of this positivists' idea of language–epistemology nexus, Quine's meaning holism with all its components that necessarily include the critique of analytic–synthetic distinction and the verificationist theory of meaning is to be understood. As stated earlier Quine's meaning holism assumes three-level structure of argument which will be presented in the following three sections.

---

[1] In my presentation of indeterminacy thesis, I have followed some of the arguments of N. Hornstein (1982).

Two Dogmas: The First Layer Argument

"Two Dogmas" presents Quine's first stage of arguments. It is of two parts. The first part consists of Quine's rejection of analyticity and the second consists of Quine's refutation of verificationism as a theory of meaning. Coming to Quine's rejection of analyticity, we have already seen how analytic–synthetic distinction gives rise to foundationalism in epistemology. Quine thus finds that rejection of foundationalism can be possible only on the basis of the rejection of analytic–synthetic distinction. His rejection of the distinction is based on the following considerations:

a. Analytic–synthetic distinction is untenable because it lacks sufficient explanatory basis.
b. The epistemological import of the distinction cannot be established unless it is adequately explained.
c. Untenability of analytic–synthetic distinction directly leads to the untenability of foundationalism.

The main thrust of Quine's critique of analyticity is an attack on the a priori. Logical positivists consider a priori knowledge is the knowledge of analytic truth. Accordingly, Quine's critique is not designed to offer a linguistic notion of analyticity but to show, on the other hand, that why we cannot have a viable epistemological notion of analyticity which can hold the foundationalism of positivism intact. There have been attempts in recent times which try to restore the analytic–synthetic distinction after the devastating attack of Quine. But in this respect, it should be kept in mind that the new definition of analyticity should do the epistemological work that tradition assigned to it, namely, ensuring a priori knowledge. Some of the researchers in linguistic semantics, for example, make the same mistake when the notion of analyticity is construed in purely linguistic term and thus its primary epistemological role is kept aside.

We will now come to Quine's critique proper and will see how some of his crucial arguments against analyticity are essentially meant to questioning the type of connection between language and epistemology that positivism assumes. In fact, positivists' construal of this relationship, as Quine's critique shows, fails to support a viable notion of analyticity. Quine's well-known argument of vicious circularity shows that viciousness that he is talking about is not formal rather viciousness arises due to the epistemological nature of the problem associates with analytic-synthetic distinction. In specific term, his claim that explication of the notion of analyticity, meaning, etc., is viciously circular because the definitions constructed for all these concepts and the concepts that they are defining presuppose the same epistemological issues. In other words, that which is to be defined and the method by which to define are subjected to the same epistemological difficulty. The result of not succeeding in defining analyticity due to its inherent circularity makes it evident that the connection between theory of meaning and theory of knowledge that positivists are talking about is untenable. This idea may be instantiated in the light of Quine's argument against analyticity in terms of synonymity and semantic rules.

Quine's strategy for defining analyticity adopted the following line of reasoning. His proposal is that analyticity can be defined in terms of cognitive synonymy which in turn can be defined in terms of interchangeability *salvaveritate.* Thus, two expressions are cognitively synonymous if they are interchangeable and this explains their reason for being analytic. To elaborate, *A* and *B* are cognitively synonymous only if *A* is substitutable for *B*. From this it follows that if *A* is cognitively synonymous with *B* then "*A* is *B*" is analytic.

Crucial to this definition is the notion of interchangeability which fits well in the context of extensional languages. To say, *A* is extensionally equivalent to *B* implies *A* is substitutable everywhere for *B* and vice versa. This is how the notion of interchangeability is formulated in extensional languages. But the difficulty with this formulation is that it does not satisfy the requirement of positivist epistemology. A definition of this sort cannot support the basic epistemological distinction that positivism makes between two notions of truth, namely; truth due to meaning and truth due to fact. The reason is that within an extensional language we cannot make such a distinction. From the point of view of extensional language, the sentence, "All bachelors are unmarried" and the sentence "All chordates are renates" may be viewed as similar because they are true and the reason for their being true is same. They are true on the ground of "accidental matters of fact", as Quine puts it. The notion of interchangeability is thus defined solely in relation to the world of facts and this is the only notion of interchangeability that an extensional language allows. But this will miserably fail to account for the distinction that the positivist theory of knowledge requires, i.e. the statements that are true by meaning and the statements that are true due to the way facts are organized in the world. It is this epistemological distinction that the notion of interchangeability defined in terms of extensional equivalence is unable to provide.

The only option thus left is to consider non-extensional language. It is a language which allows the distinction between interchangeability in extensional contexts (where predicates are extensionally equivalent) and interchangeability in modal context (where predicates are equivalent necessarily and not due to any actual accident). This is the way how positivists' requirement can be fulfilled. It is through the intervention of necessity operator truths of meaning are distinguished from mere contingent truths as expressed through extensional equivalence. The expression "necessarily" thus implies the context where only the predicates which are necessarily and not contingently true can be interchanged. The resources of modal language thus enable us to reformulate the two sentences in the following way. The sentence "A chordate is a renate" is certainly true but it is contingently true since the equivalence is based on the agreement of fact, whereas the sentence "A bachelor is an unmarried man" cannot be other than being true and hence it is always read as: "It is necessarily true that a bachelor is an unmarried man". On the basis of the resources of modal language a notion of interchangeability can be so defined that it will fulfil the requirement of positivist epistemology.

But then Quine questions this reformulation suggested on the basis of the consideration of modal language. His main criticism is that properties of this language are as problematic as the notion of analyticity which is now placed within the necessity operator of modal language. In fact, Quine states that both necessity and analyticity have the same set of problems. That means the defect that is noticed in one can be equally noticed in another. The reason is that one cannot be defined independently of the other. To elaborate, the notion of "necessity" cannot be explained independently of the notion of "analyticity". The two statements "Necessarily *A* is *B*" and " '*A* is *B*' is analytic" have the same epistemological problem. Their mutual dependence can be evidently seen once we take these two notions together. For to decide whether the statement "*A* is *B*" is necessarily true ultimately depends on whether the statement is analytic or not. Thus, analyticity is defined in terms of interchangeability based on the modal notion of necessity and which in turn is defined in terms of analyticity. This way the definition of analyticity becomes inevitable and viciously circular when construed in modal language.

Similarly, Carnap's attempt to define analyticity in terms of semantic rules construed in a formal language is equally defective. Carnap's plea is that a statement *S* is analytic if and only if it follows from the semantical or syntactical rules of the language. The obvious advantage here is that since rules are explicitly stated, one could, on the basis of that, be able to define the notion of analyticity. But the notion of analyticity to be defined here will not be a general notion of analyticity. It will only be a definition of analyticity for a specific language say *L*. Quine's point is that such a definition does not serve any epistemological purpose is similar to the notion of interchangeability. This attempt too involves the charge of circularity.

In the positivists' project, the task of epistemology consists in logically reconstructing the sentences of theory into those that are grounded in the linguistic framework and those that are not so grounded. Now this procedure can work only when there exists already a criterion for dividing a theory into sentences that are related to the framework and the sentences that are not. Without such a criterion, we cannot judge whether the reconstruction is correct or not. The construction will be correct if it clearly demarcates the analytical statements of the system to be true due to the nature of semantical rules and the contingent statements whose truths are not determined by any such rules. But the knowledge of this can be obtained only when we have a general notion of analyticity that defines *S* as analytic in *L* for variable *S* and *L*. In the absence of such a general notion, a distinction between two types of statements cannot be made. Why is it that the availability of such a general notion of analyticity so important? In a particular reconstruction, semantical rules are constituted with a certain epistemological distinction and thus they cannot define such a distinction. For analyticity to be epistemologically important it must not be defined in terms of any given language. In fact, it should be prior to any such language. Without this, analyticity will turn into a declarative notion having no epistemological significance whatsoever.[2] As a result, the whole problem of deciding whether semantical rules in a particular reconstruction correctly characterize all on only analytic statements remains unanswered and unexplained. This way the attempt to define analyticity in terms of semantical rules involves vicious circularity. Analyticity and semantical rules are so interdependent that one cannot be defined without the other.

The above discussion shows that language–epistemology nexus of positivism is inherently defective. The main source of its weakness lies in its conception of language. One of its major assumptions is that language is viewed independently of the

---

[2] Carnap 1952.

experience of the world. As a result, a rigid distinction is created between language, on the one hand, and the world, on the other. This distinction is responsible for giving rise to the dichotomy between two notions of truth, i.e. truth by virtue of meaning and truth by virtue of experience. Quine's rejection of this distinction rests on his fundamental thesis that there is no separate place for linguistic component vis-à-vis our conceptual scheme due to which we can have truth by virtue of the linguistic component alone.

The next is the assumption central to language–epistemology nexus of positivism, i.e. the primacy of sentence over language. Sentences are taken to be independent units in a language which are true or false on their own. Sentences are thus not seen as forming a system expressing a totality. This gives rise to atomistic picture of language which is to a large extent responsible for the analytic–synthetic dichotomy. The atomistic picture of language is a well-established tradition in contemporary Western philosophy defended by Russell, Early Wittgenstein, Carnap and so on. Quine's rejection of analytic–synthetic distinction thus presupposes the rejection of the atomistic view of language which is replaced by the view that language and conceptual scheme together form a holistic system.

Two Dogmas: The Second Layer Argument

With atomistic picture of language we may now come to Quine's critique of verificationist theory of meaning through which he shows how meaning works holistically. Verificationism is an account according to which the meaning of a sentence is the method of empirically confirming or disconfirming it. Analytic sentences are of course kept separately since they are confirmed "no matter what" or "come what may". This may be viewed as another way — a procedure through which analytic–synthetic distinction can be ascertained via verificationist theory of meaning. A sentence will be called analytic if it is confirmed no matter what. Otherwise, the sentence will be synthetic. This way of arguing will make sense only if we accept verificationist account of meaning to be correct. The basic thrust of Quine's critique is to show that the verificationist theory of meaning is wrong. It is wrong not on any other ground, such as, circularity. It is wrong because the account of meaning that it offers is false.

Verificationism has its root in reductionism of the earlier positivist work, such as, the *Aufbau* project of Carnap.[3] True, verificationism does not subscribe to radical reductionism but, nevertheless, it assumes in its account of meaning a subtler form of reductionist thesis. The reason is, Quine points out, verificationism holds the following theses: First, for each synthetic statement there corresponds a set of possible sensory events, and second, occurrence of any one of them will establish the truth or falsity of the sentence concerned. From this Quine concludes that verificationism retains reductionist element because it shares with reductionism that each statement is confirmed or disconfirmed in isolation from other sentences. Verificationism in this sense embraces reductionism.

Quine's historic objection to this account is that this is not the way how theories confront the world. As against the verificationist stand, Quine puts forward his well-known thesis that sentences do not meet experience one by one but as "corporate body". The theory as a whole is what matters when it interacts with experience. This is where Quine sharply differs from verificationist understanding of the composition of a theory. In verificationist account, a theory is an additive concept because a theory is understood as consisting of individual sentences. They are like parts and a theory is a summation of these parts. The Duhem–Quine thesis rejects this view of verificationists. They viewed that a theory as a whole cannot be identified with the mere summation of its parts, namely, the individual sentences. A theory is far more than such a summation. In this regard, the positivists' idea of sentences having meaning individually is no longer tenable. The failure of verificationism

[3] Carnap 1947.

arises due to its wrong notion of theory and its relationship with the world.

Duhem points out that the physicist can never subject an isolated hypothesis to experimental test, but only a whole group of hypotheses. When the experiment is in disagreement with his predictions, what he learns is that at least one of the hypotheses constituting this group is unacceptable and ought to be modified; but the experiment does not disagree with which one should be changed.[4] Duhem's thesis is specific to hypothesis of physics. He states that experiments are to be confirmed or unconfirmed and take place within a group of hypotheses. Deviating from Duhem, but not completely, Quine expresses that what confirms or conflicts within a group of hypotheses are not due to the results of experiments but due to the persuasion of sense-experiences. Here Quine goes ahead of Duhem by viewing that Duhem's model of meaning holism delimits its scope within the sphere of physics. Hence, he expresses that even a statement very close to the periphery (of our field of beliefs) can be held true in the face of recalcitrant experience by pleading hallucination (TDE/Duhem 1962: 43).

Quine in his *Word and Object* states that the talk of sense-experience gives way to talk of stimuli. From this, he brings in the notion "stimulus meaning" into the discussion.[5] There are two sorts of stimulus meaning.

1. Affirmative stimulus meaning (ASM).
2. Negative stimulus meaning (NSM).

He defines ASM as the class of all stimulations that would prompt a speaker's assent and NSM is the class of all stimulations that would prompt his dissent.[6] The stimulus meaning of a speaker comprises of the ordered pair of its affirmative and negative stimulus meanings. Thus, he asserts that sentences about the

[4] This concept is borrowed from Duhem 1962: 187.

[5] Please see Quine 1960b.

[6] Ibid.: 32.

external world cannot be assigned stimulus meaning one-by-one, but only collectively, in sets.[7] In his words:

> I did intend the stimulus meaning to capture the notion of meaning for the linguistic community in the case of an observation sentence, and for the individual speaker in the case of many other occasion sentences.[8]

In conglomeration of Duhem and Quine's view on epistemological nature of meaning, the theses have given a combined view that the falsity of the observation categorical does not conclusively refute the hypothesis:

> What it refutes is the conjunction of sentences that was needed to imply the observation categorical. In order to retract that conjunction we do not have to retract the hypothesis in question; we could retract some other sentences of the conjunction instead. — Quine 1990: 13-14

Thus, according to Quine,

> no statement, taken in isolation from its fellows, admits confirmation at all. Our statements face the tribunal of sense-experience only as a corporate body. Hence, he says, it is not significant, in general, to speak of the confirmation of a single statement.[9]

The Duhem–Quine view of theory thus does not provide support to the notion of analyticity that positivist theory of epistemology requires. The reason is, it is not the sentence but the language that matters in deciding truth. There is a clear break from the atomistic view of language to the holistic view of language. Accordingly, the Carnapian distinction between the cognitive and the practical or between the internal questions and the external questions does not find any place in this holistic picture of language. There is

---

[7] Hale and Wright 1999: 23.

[8] Quine 1986: 427-28.

[9] Wagner 1986: 1.

nothing like linguistic choice and cognitive choice to be conceived separately. All choices involved are both linguistic and cognitive. There is no epistemological vantage point on which to ground analytic–synthetic distinction.

However, Quine's " has a problem. In spite of its strength and boldness, it is incomplete as a critique to establish that meaning works holistically. Quine's critique lacks substantial arguments stating why verificationism is wrong. It claims that verificationism is wrong because it presupposes a wrong view regarding the relationship between language and the world. One can very well challenge this and may point out that Quine's claim that sentences do not face experience individually but as a corporate body is unfounded. We do not simply see such an event happening. What will be Quine's reply to this? In constructive terms, we need to know first, where exactly the verificationist account of meaning breaks down. Second, is there any good reason that compels us to reject verificationism as a theory of meaning? And, third, what is the crucial aspect in a theory construction that cannot be accounted for in verificationist theory of meaning? In this respect, Quine's thesis on the indeterminacy of translation can be of enormous help. It completes the argument that Quine started in his critique on verificationism. It provides answers to the three questions raised above. It may not be inappropriate to say that one of the interpretations of the indeterminacy thesis is to show that verificationist account of meaning fails epistemologically. With this, we may now come to the indeterminacy thesis which constitutes the third layer of argument in Quine's proposal on meaning holism.

Indeterminacy of Translation: Quine's Third Layer Argument

In view of the issues raised in the previous presentation, we may now discuss the indeterminacy thesis with a view to complete Quine's critique of verificationism. Considering this, we shall focus on the three issues. First, the translation scenario as posed by the thesis. Second, the epistemological reconstruction of the thesis which accounts for the issues unexplained in Quine's critique. And third, the epistemological status of the distinction between truth by language and truth by fact in the light of indeterminacy thesis.

THE TRANSLATION SCENARIO

The scenario presented by the indeterminacy thesis is the story of a field linguist who is strongly inclined towards behaviouristic approach to language. He goes into an alien community to translate a language about which he does not have any knowledge. For him, to make translation the only option remains to rely on stimulus meaning. It is through this notion of stimulus meaning that he is able to correlate sentences of his language with sentences of the native language. Thus, the possibility of translation implies equivalence in terms of stimulus meaning which is correlated with certain environmental stimulation. Apart from his access to stimulus meaning, the linguist is also given access to the native's version of "yes" and "no" on the basis of which he will be able to identify affirmative stimulus meaning and negative stimulus meaning. These are the tools available to the linguist and the problem posed here is that how the linguist can be successful in his translation by relying solely on these tools. Of course, if meanings of sentences are determined individually, then there is no reason for him to be unsuccessful.

In this connection, the three types of sentences[10] that matter to the linguist are:

(i) occasion sentences (i.e. the sentences that are close to environmental conditions);

(ii) complex truth functional sentences; and

(iii) standing sentences (the sentences that are not directly connected to observation).

The linguist does not have any problem while translating

[10] Quine 1961.

occasion sentences and truth functional sentences. But difficulty arises when he deals with the standing sentences. The main difficulty that arises here is that since standing sentences are situated far away from environmental stimulation, stimulus meaning cannot be of much help. It is found to be inadequate because it cannot account for the cognitive meaning of these sentences. Here Quine[11] introduced his proposal called "interanimation of sentences". It is a proposal which makes it explicit the process through which standing sentences are related to experience. Since these sentences cannot be directly related to experience, they need a mediator — the intervening sentences. As Quine has spelt out the process, standing sentences are related to experience by virtue of getting related to other sentences. This is how sentences are interanimated, i.e. associating sentences with other sentences. It is precisely at this point — when sentences are interanimated — stimulus meaning breaks down. The linguist finds that he has to go upward. His available tools will not help him. This new scenario arises due to the following reasons. Interanimation or relating sentences to one another assumes a procedure with the following steps. First, sentences must be broken into parts (i.e. words) and second, these parts must be related to what they designate. This involves constructing a grammar which will specify the above procedure. The problem that the linguist faces here is that this cannot be done within the available means of stimulus meaning. Words (i.e. the parts of sentences) may be related to the same object in different ways depending on the nature of circumstances. The same stimulus situation pertaining to an object may give rise to different interpretations of the object, such as, an undetached object part, an instance of objecthood and so on. From this, two important conclusions follow: stimulus meaning by itself cannot account for the different ways that words are related to objects, and further, because of this lack of determinate relationship existing between

[11] Quine 1961: 38.

words and objects, stimulus meaning cannot provide the basis for fixing the referential apparatus. It is at this point of translation situation when the linguist finds that the cognitive meaning of a sentence depends on the relation with other sentences, he feels the urge to go beyond stimulus meaning and introduces analytical hypotheses. In Quine's own admission, through stimulus meaning we will never be able to determine first "what are terms" and "what terms are coextensive".[12]Hence, to make translation the linguist has to inevitably fall back on analytical hypotheses which though are not methodologically allowed to him. With this scenario, we can now go to the second problem suggesting an epistemological construal of the indeterminacy thesis.

EPISTEMOLOGICAL CONSTRUAL OF INDETERMINACY THESIS

The basic formulation of indeterminacy thesis, though presented in linguistic term, can be recast in such a way that its epistemological significance can be brought out in relation to verificationism. With all probability, it can be argued that behaviourist theory of meaning is an expression of verificationism. In our earlier discussion, we have seen that in behaviourism the meaning of a sentence is taken to be equivalent with the environmental stimulus associated with the sentence. Behaviourism thus advocates that sentences attain their meaning individually. We give meaning to individual sentences in isolation from the rest. This is the aspect on which both the accounts of meaning — behaviourism and verificationism — converge. On the basis of this convergence, one can argue in a general way that if verificationism is shown to be false, then on the same consideration the behaviourist theory of meaning can be found to be equally defective, if not false. This is conspicuous in the context of radical translation, which fails to provide a general account of meaning because of its dependence on behaviouristic principles. The main reason for the failure of verificationism and behaviourism is that both subscribe to a

[12] Quine 1961: 41-42.

wrong view — a view concerning how sentences are related to the world. They share the same presupposition that the meaning of a sentence can be determined in isolation from the other sentences of the language. That is the reason, the ground on which radical translation conceived within the compulsions of stimulus meaning fails. It is on the same consideration verificationist account of meaning fails too. It is the atomistic view of language, i.e. where sentences confronting the world individually are responsible for the failure of behaviourism and verificationism as a theory of meaning.

In this respect, one may specially mention here the identical nature of the principle that governs grammar construction and theory construction based on behaviourist principle and verificationist notion of meaning. This will enable us to see how both of them share the same defect. The problem found in grammar construction in behaviourism has its parallel in the epistemological account of theory construction in positivism. This is particularly reflected in its distinction between truths of language and truths of the world.

We have seen that translation works well with occasion sentences and truth functions. These are the contexts where the meanings of sentences can be determined by directly correlating them with environmental stimulations. At this stage, the behaviourist–verificationist account of meaning can be taken as constituting a viable theory of cognitive content of low-level occasion sentences and truth functions. But problem arises when interanimation becomes a crucial factor for successful translation. It is realized that the verificationist notion like stimulus meaning cannot function any more. At this stage, the meaning of a sentence is given indirectly as the function of the meaning of the parts. Giving internal structure to the sentences becomes important since a sentence is made up of smaller meaningful units. This consists of grammar construction which goes beyond the scope of stimulus meaning.

A similar scenario is found in the positivist notion of verificationism. In the light of indeterminacy thesis, we can see what is wrong with verificationism of the positivist variety. Since stimulus meaning and verificationist notion of meaning are not substantially different, both of them are unable to account for interanimation of grammar which essentially implies the system relating words to objects. In this respect verificationism too has the same problem as that of stimulus meaning. Within the verificationist set-up there is no provision for giving sentences one set of semantic rules rather than another. Verificationism should be thus supplemented by analytical hypotheses which will allow us to see how sentences are related to the world holistically. In order to give a holistic turn to verificationist theory it needs to be reconstructed so that internal structure of sentences can be accounted for. This is necessary in order to give account of the cognitive nature of the high-level sentences of scientific theory.

TRUTHS OF LANGUAGE AND TRUTHS OF THE WORLD

In the positivist theory of language since the cognitive meaning of a sentence is determined in isolation from the rest of language, a peculiar distinction is implicitly maintained between language and sentences. The cognitive meaning of a sentence becomes the primary one and the language to which it belongs becomes derivative. In the light of analytical hypotheses, we can say that this distinction is false. For to give cognitive meaning of sentences, the notion of language must be presupposed. Meaning becomes derivative in this conception since it is derived from language or grammar. Choice of grammar, i.e. analytical hypotheses, is based on empirical consideration.[13] Analytical hypotheses are the ones through which cognitive meaning of sentences is accounted for. The choice of language thus becomes crucial for cognitive meaning. In this sense, choice of language has a cognitive import.

[13] Quine 1960b: 70.

This choice is no longer then non-empirical. If choice of language is empirical then the positivist distinction between truths of language and the truths of the world becomes untenable.

7

Davidson and Meaning Holism

The truth-conditional approach to language plays a vital role when we attempt to explore what the theory of meaning is about. It is stated that to know the meaning of a sentence means to know its truth-value, i.e. under what conditions the sentence will be treated as true or false. Hence, knowing the meaning of a sentence implies understanding the sentence. Supporting this view Davidson explains that each proposition can be treated as either true or false because each proposition has a specific sense and it is intrinsically related to the state of affairs of the world. If the sense of a proposition maps the state of affairs of the world then the proposition will be judged as true and if it does not, then the proposition will be treated as false.

On the view of Davidson, theory of meaning can be treated same as theory of understanding. He reasons that to understand a proposition we must know what it states about. That explains how the nature of meaning and the facts of the world or the states of affairs existing in the world are closely connected. This may be explained in detail if we analyse the following issues:

1. How do we understand a sentence?
2. How do we know what the sentence is about?
3. What makes communication possible?
4. What is it for a word or expression to be meaningful?
5. How do the meanings of the complex expressions in a language depend upon their parts?

In relation to the above issues, Davidson incorporates a few other conditions such as:

1. How can a theory of truth provide us a theory of meaning?
2. How does a theory of truth yield interpretations of statements?
3. What is it required for a theory to be empirically verifiable?

All these issues revolve around a vital and significant inquiry, i.e. "what is a theory of meaning and how is it related to truth-value?" Attempting to answer this query Davidson delineates that the task of constructing a theory which gives the extension of the truth predicate of a language implies the task of showing how from a finite number of axioms and procedural rules we can deduce the infinite number of theorems that give the truth conditions for the sentence of a language.[1] From this, a question may be raised: "what it is for a sentence to be true?" Responding to this question, Quine says, if we equate meaning with empirical content and insist that only theories as a whole have empirical content then sentences have meanings only as parts of a body of a theory. In such a body it is possible to systematically tamper with the roles assigned to its parts in ways that leave the empirical content of the theory as a whole unaltered.[2] In this context, he argues that it is not possible to fix the meaning of any individual sentence by referring to our experiences.

While discussing the theory of meaning in relation to truth, it is noticed that Davidson is influenced by Quine's work on "radical translation". He has borrowed this idea from Quine and developed his own theory "radical interpretation" for establishing the theory of meaning holism. It was Quine who first gave the three seminal ideas, i.e. holism, indeterminacy and charity which became central to Davidson's theory of interpretation.

---

[1] Please see Davidson 1984a.

[2] This concept is borrowed from Quine 1960.

It is further noticed that Quine had not worked out explicitly the interconnection between these three concepts. But Davidson has brought out the full implications of these three concepts while developed his theory of interpretation. In his theory of interpretation, he reorganized these three ideas and developed a holistic conception of interpretation in the light of the other two ideas — indeterminacy and charity.

However, distinguishing himself from Quine, Davidson expresses that we do not need an epistemological bridge between language and the world because language is not a filter or a screen through which knowledge of the world must pass.[3] So, according to him, theory of meaning is decided by theory of truth that envisages whether a particular proposition is meaningful or not. Therefore, each and every sentence would be judged as either true or false. While discussing the theory of meaning he incorporates the following issues. These are: theory of interpretation, theory of truth, principle of charity and the network of belief system.

This chapter deals with a detailed presentation of the exposition of the Davidsonian theory of meaning with a view to find out the semantic nature of a language, i.e. how meaning works holistically. To start with the theory that meaning functions holistically Davidson took the help of Tarski's view of *T*-schema where Tarski emphatically expresses that "a (finite) theory *T* is a truth theory for language *L* iff, for each sentence *E* of *L*, *T* entails a *T*-sentence of the form":

E is true-in-*L* iff *P*.[4]

This theory is taken to be considered as extensionally adequate iff all the *T*-sentences it entails are true. On this account, Jerry Fodor and Ernest Lepore evoke the holistic approach to meaning advocates that for "any expression to have even reasonably

---

[3] This view is derived from the Davidsonean analysis on "Interpretative Theory", please see Ramberg 1984.

[4] The analysis is found in Fordor and Lepore 1992: 60.

deterministic content, there must be other contentful expressions that belong to the same linguistic system as it does" (Fodor and Lepore 1992: 69).

Tarski in his truth theory says that a formal definition of the truth predicate as it applies within a language *L* can be given with reference to meta-language *M* by providing for every sentence *S* of *L*, a matching sentence in *M* which is translationally synonymous with *S*. This requirement is known as "Convention *T*". Further, to understand this notion we have to know the material adequacy condition of truth definition.

Conditions of Material Adequacy

A definition of truth ought to be such that it defines all that is truth and nothing that falls under it is not truth. Not only this but it should also capture the intuitive notion of truth. The material adequacy condition aims at securing all these. The material adequacy condition is given in terms of "Convention *T*" which states that the definition of truth for a language *L* is correct iff we are able to deduce a sentence (*T*-sentence) from the schema called *T*-schema available for every sentence of that language which is: "*X* is true iff *P*". Here *X* is replaced by a structural descriptive name of a sentence say *S*, and *P* is replaced by a correct translation of *S* into the meta-language (i.e. the language of the truth theory). For Example, " 'Snow is white' is true iff snow is white". This asserts that Tarski's theory confines within the boundary of reference and truth conditions.

Davidson does not restrict himself to the Tarskian model of truth theory because he aims at establishing the theory of meaning which can be applicable to all languages including natural language. To do so, he states that when we derive the meaning of a sentence the *T*-sentences of it are meant to match the sentence of the object language with a sentence in the meta-language in a way that the latter is a correct translation of the former. Therefore, the sentence in the meta-language gives us the meaning of the sentence of the object language. It is so because being a correct translation of the sentence of the object language it retains the same meaning. Hence, the *T*-sentences give us the specification of meanings. Moreover, we have to note that the manner in which we arrive at *T*-sentences by deriving them from the definition does not involve the concept of meaning and still the definition along with the derivational system ensures the matching of sentences of the object language with sentences of the meta-language which have the same meaning. One may say that the concept of meaning via the concept of translation has been used in laying down the condition of material adequacy. But this does not lead to any kind of circularity as the condition of material adequacy is neither part of the definition of truth nor of any such derivational system is associated with it. It is simply an external check to ensure the correctness of the definition of truth.

In this regard, Davidson states that mastery of a theory of meaning is same as the mastery of a language for which the theory is formulated. A theory, on his view, lays down a systematic way of determining the meaning of all the significant expressions of a language. Hence, a theory of meaning is supposed to lay down the most general conditions to be considered as a satisfactory theory. A satisfactory theory of meaning gives an account of how meanings of sentences depend upon the meanings of words. A legible theory for a semantic determination of truth conditions of all statements provides the conditions under which a sentence will be treated as true or false. Thus, a theory of truth for a language *L* must be such that:

a. For each sentence *S* of *L* a *T*-sentence should be provable.

b. Each of such provable *T*-sentence should be true.

These two basic principles together explain the material adequacy of truth that explains the underlying conditions under which a sentence will be judged as either true or false. For example, "'Snow is white' is true if and only if snow is white".

Proceeding further, Davidson says that Tarski's *T*-schema has its own limitations because it is applicable to only logically perfect language or formal language. It cannot be applicable to all other languages. Hence, there might be a question regarding how to determine the truth-value of a *T*-sentence of ordinary language. But we could not also claim that sentences of ordinary language are irrelevant because of their incapability of determining their truth-value and, therefore we must omit them from the language system. To overcome this lacuna, Davidson gives an alternative solution of finding a truth theory which will be a stronger and valid one for determining the meaning of a proposition.

Davidson's entire project on truth theory is based on two fundamental objectives.

First: Constructing a theory of truth which will be applicable to natural languages based on the Tarskian model of Convention-*T*.

Second: Constructing a theory of meaning and interpretation for natural languages modelled on the theory of truth constructed at the first stage.

These two objectives summarize the Davidsonean approach to meaning, i.e. how meaning works holistically in a language.

The prior analysis signifies that the theory of truth and the theory of meaning are interdependent and therefore we can claim that the theory of meaning for a language is essentially involved with the theory of truth. In this perspective, Davidson claims that there can be *T*-sentences available for natural languages if it satisfies the indexical principle, i.e. time and place. For example, the *T*-sentence for a sentence, such as:

"I am hungry".

It will be,

(*T*) "I am hungry" is true spoken by *P* at time *t* if and only if *P* is hungry at time *t*. In this manner, *T*-sentences are available in relation to a particular speaker and time. The task of Convention-*T* as stated earlier is to give an account of the meaning of a sentence and the truth conditions of a sentence. For him, the determination of the meaning of a sentence and the truth-value of that sentence is so closely connected that one cannot be differentiated from the other. Thus, it is viewed that a truth theory while explaining truth also explains meaning. The knowledge of truth conditions may be thus characterized as the knowledge of the semantic conditions of truth. This essentially involves knowing what it is for a sentence to be true which implies understanding the language.

It has been stated earlier that there cannot be any understanding of the language without understanding the meaning. Since the theory of truth is essentially related to the theory of meaning on this ground that the theory of truth is related to the theory of understanding, an equation is thus established between meaning, truth and understanding. In this respect, Davidson's idea of truth theory being empirically significant expresses truth theory's commitment to meaning. As he says, for a truth theory to be empirically significant, all the *T*-sentences of it must be supported by linguistic evidences.

With respect to the second objective he states that theory of interpretation plays a vital role for understanding the meaning of a proposition. On his view, to determine the meaning of a proposition is to interpret the proposition in various possible ways. Hence, his submission is that a theory of meaning must be regarded as a theory of interpretation.

Theory of Meaning as a Theory of Interpretation

One way of seeing how a truth theory involves a theory of interpretation is to see what a field linguist has to do when he encounters a new language. He first formulates a theory and then tests the correctness of the theory. In forming a theory of interpretation, which is in fact an empirical theory, the field linguist has to depend upon the utterances or the prompted assents made by the native speaker in a particular situation. These utterances or prompted assents or dissents are actually an action performed by the native speaker — an action which is determined by many factors.

i. The meaning the native speaker assigns to the sentence.

ii. The belief that the native speaker entertains in the situation.

iii. The desire the speaker has in the situation.

To find out a right interpretation of speech of the native speaker we have to find out the meanings that the native assigns to the uttered or assented sentences. In order to search for this we have to take the above-mentioned three factors into account. In this connection, even if we know the value of any two of the three factors as represented in the form of argument we can know the value of the third argument. Let us find out what kind of belief and desire we can assign to the native speaker on the occasion of his/her assent or dissent to an utterance of a sentence. An example will clarify how the notion of interpretation works in actual situation.

Assume *X* as a non-Andhrite detained in a village of Andhra Pradesh, a southern state of India where no one knows any language other than Telugu. The person *X* is staying in a house where he finds a beautiful girl who appears to be very lean and weak enters into the premise. The house owner by seeing her asks "bagunava"? *X* presumes that the house owner is praising her beauty as *X* entertains the same belief when he meets any beautiful girl. Further, *X* finds that when an old person comes to the house the house owner says "bagunava" to him. *X* on the basis of this incidents interprets "bagunava" in the following way, "bagunava" is uttered by the owner of the house is true iff someone is weak. But *X* is surprised when in the next morning a young man comes to that house who is very healthy and the house owner asks "bagunava". Then *X* concludes that he is in interpreting "bagunava" as either "beauty" or "weak". *X* could then assumes that "bagunava" means "how are you?" So in this case *X* ought to take the native speaker to be at least as rational as he is. In this case the first alternative and the second alternative vary from each other. So *X* has to find out some other common characteristics which force him to conclude that:

"Bagunava" is true iff it means how are you.

This asserts that while going through all the assumptions and their verification, we come to know most of the axioms of the Telugu language and hence we can derive the theorems of meaning theory for Telugu which are nothing but the *T*-sentences of Telugu language.

Now a question arises: how do we know that the *T*-sentences or the meaning theorems are true? An answer may be given that one has to relate the truth theory to actual linguistic practice of the native speaker. This creates another problem, i.e. how can we do so? How can we provide empirical content to the truth theory to make it sensitive to the practices of the native speaker? This question arises because we find the native speakers try to relate empirical evidences in their linguistic practices. Further, a question may be raised: is the truth theory that once related to our linguistic practice can act like a meaning theory?

To know that a theory is correct is to know either (a) the axioms of the theory are correct by being empirically testified, or (b) each of the derivations of the theory, i.e. the *T*-sentences are testified by experience and are thus true. Davidson does not show his inclination towards the first alternative because it may lead to the atomistic theory of meaning where each sentence is self-sufficient for determining its truth-value. If he had suggested this theory for determining the truth-value of a sentence, his theory wouldn't be considered as a satisfactory one for determining the truth-value of the sentences of natural language. Thus, he preferred the second alternative where we have to ascertain the deliverances of the theory, i.e. the *T*-sentences are true or are corroborated by the actual linguistic practice of the native speaker. In order to find out the truth of a *T*-sentence we have to find out whether all the other *T*-sentences following from the theory are true or not, and are being corroborated by linguistic practice. This inevitably leads to meaning holism. It states that the only way in which we may know the meaning of a sentence is by knowing the true *T*-sentence of it.

But to know the *T*-sentence we have to know all other *T*-sentences that follow from the theory are true, i.e. the meanings of all other *T*-sentences have to be known. We cannot know the meaning of any sentence in isolation from other sentences. Thus, to know the meaning of a sentence we have to know the meaning of all other sentences of a language within a particular paradigm.

This analysis raises an issue, i.e. how are we going to know that the theory yields consequences which are corroborated by the linguistic practice of the native speaker? We have to find out whether the native speaker does take the *T-sentence* in question to be the meaning-specifying sentence. That means, does it specify the meaning of the sentence whose meaning we are trying to find out? What we are trying to do is to give a correct interpretation of the bit of linguistic behaviour of the native speaker. And the interpretation of the bit of linguistic behaviour may be seen as a redescription of the following kind:

From: Susama has uttered the sentence "Varshaheuchhi".

To: Susama has said that it is raining.

Now the question is, what do we need to know if we are to be in a position to redescribe the utterance in this way? We have to know:

a. The circumstance of the utterance of the sentence "Varshaheuchhi" by Susama, i.e. we have to find out that it is indeed raining.
b. It is in the circumstance of rain that Susama makes the utterance "Varshaheuchhi".
c. Susama as a rule maker of the utterance "Varshaheuchhi" utters in the circumstance of rain, and all native speakers of Odiya language in such a circumstance utter or assent to the sentence "Varshaheuchhi". (And this should be established strongly enough to be able to handle counterfactuals like: Someone who is not a native speaker of Odiya would have given assent to "Varshaheuchhi" in the circumstance of rain.)

In this regard, a crucial issue for Davidson is to find out the rational grounds on the basis of which we can decide the indefinite *T*-theories that are extensionally adequate representations of a language *L* and it is to be identified as the correct meaning theory for the language *L*.

Along with his theory of interpretation Davidson introduces the notion "radical interpretation" which has two functions.[5]

a. It must specify the kinds of empirical evidence that a successful meaning theory is required to account for.
b. Since different ways of constraining the evidence will lead to different *T*-theories, a radical interpretation theory must justify the imposition of one set of evidential constraints in preference to others.

By explaining the term "empirical evidence", Davidson states that it includes any contingent propositions that the radical interpreter may legitimately appeal to warrant his interpretation.[6] Thus for him, *T*-theory is to be selected on the basis of "evidence plausibly available to an interpreter" where an interpreter is "someone who does not already know how to interpret utterances the theory is designed to cover" (Davidson 1984a: 128; Fodor and Lepore 1992: 72).

In this regard, Davidson states that a successful meaning theory is one where the meaning of an expression must provide an extensionally adequate truth theory and it meets further evidential constraints. In the context of radical interpretation, the primary question raised is: "How is it the case that whatever the native said to the field linguist in the behavioural form, the field linguist would receive it in the same form or same spirit?" Further, it may be asked what characteristics the field linguist must have to understand the behavioural approach of the natives? Again, is there any guarantee that the field linguist possesses the required features what he needs to understand the natives' behaviour?

---

[5] These two features are borrowed from ibid.: 71.

[6] Ibid.

To resolve all these problems Davidson introduces the notion of "network of belief". According to him, there are two sorts of belief, "network of belief" and "dense pattern of belief". Meaning and belief form a nexus in case of "network of belief". But in case of "dense pattern of belief" meaning and belief are conjoined and forms an agreement pattern, i.e. the maximum agreement between meaning of a proposition and the belief form. He further subsumes that beliefs form a "belief system". Ascribing the belief system Quine enunciates that any utterances can be considered as language if it arouses the possibility of radical interpretation. This asserts "nothing can be a language unless the correct *T*-theory for it could be selected by the sorts of observations plausibly available to the child or the linguist" (Fodor and Lepore 1992: 73). Endorsing this view Davidson says, "a child learns his first words and sentences by hearing and using them in the presence of appropriate stimuli" (Fodor and Lepore 1992: 72). Thus, it is stated that both a child and the linguist do succeed in choosing the right meaning theory on the basis of evidences available to them. Hence for both of them, meaning is to be identified as cognitive meaning.

A question may arise, what is the significance of the "theory of interpretation" in the context of theory of meaning? Attempting to answer this question Davidson iterates that the aim of the "theory of interpretation" is to interpret the language of other speakers and in addition to it he assumes that an interpreter is one who seeks to understand what other speakers mean when they utter something. Adding further, he conveys that it is necessary for an interpreter to identify the conditions under which a speaker holds true occasion sentences by judging his/her beliefs.

In an interpretative theory regarding the issue concerning how communication takes place between the hearer and the speaker Davidson says that it becomes possible only when it satisfies the following features or requirements:[7]

[7] These two issues are borrowed from Ludwig 1999: 43.

a. To have a belief, one must have the concept of a belief.

b. To have the concept of a belief, one must have the concept of error or equivalently of objective truth.

c. The claim that a being has the concept of objective truth stands in need of grounding, in particular, there must be scope for the application of the concept in the being's experience.

There are three conditions of interpretation through which we can understand the role and significance of interpretation in the construction of a theory of truth empirically. They are:

a. Both interpreter and the speaker belong to the same speech community.

b. None of them must not pretend in their utterances.

c. Both of them must share a system of common beliefs.

The first one states that if the utterances of a speaker are based on his/her attitudes then we face the problem of equally eligible rival interpretations. This leads to the failure of developing a single theory of interpretation. But Davidson's claim is that to interpret a particular utterance we necessarily require a single theory of interpretation which will be comprehensive enough, so that the theory can interpret infinite number of utterances (Dasgupta 1999: 308). The main focus here is on the notion of evidence. For a theory to be comprehensive it is to be assumed that the evidence for interpretation does not change. Thus Davidson claims that the evidence for the interpretation of a particular sentence will be same for the interpretation of all utterances of a speaker or community at large. This is the reason why Davidson introduces the notion of speech community which implies speaker belonging to the same language have the same linguistic repertoire. By virtue of this speakers of the same language mean the same thing by their utterances.

The second condition of interpretation suggests that it is an essential assumption for all the speakers belonging to the same speech community that they share a similar pattern of intention. This implies that one need not pretend to others while conveying something. If they do then the problem remains as the native speaker and the interpreter fail to share their language with each other. This conveys the message that we must have a coherent interpretation. The third condition emphasizes the need for possessing a common system of beliefs between the speakers and the interpreters. Davidson calls it "shareability of belief".

Shareability of Belief

Davidson argues that there is a common system of beliefs which we share along with other speakers belonging to the same linguistic community. Thus the beliefs that I hold are roughly the same beliefs that the other speaker holds. For him, shareability of belief is a fact which is often unnoticed by us. In fact, in our everyday life we understand each other, communicate with each other, and even disagree with each other. This shows that we share most of our beliefs. In the absence of shareability of beliefs communication will be impossible. For example, when two people disagree with each other on a certain fact we see only the differences but we do not see the common ground that they share. It is this common ground which makes their disagreement possible. Hence, a disagreement also presupposes a system of commonly shared beliefs.

> An important fact about belief is that a belief is never seen in isolation from other beliefs because it is always supported by a dense pattern of beliefs. It is within this pattern or system the particular belief is identified and described. —Dasgupta 1999: 309

In Davidson's account, belief plays an important role for determining the meanings of utterances of a speaker. Meanings of utterances of a speaker are determined by three conditions. First, by assigning his/her beliefs to the sentences by the interpreter; second, by holding his/her belief to be true; and the third, by supposing his/

her intention must be good[8] while uttering the sentences. These three are the tasks of an interpreter so as to interpret the language of the other speakers.

The above-mentioned three conditions claim that one can understand the meanings of the speaker's utterances. Further, Davidson argues that in assigning belief to others we go by the principle of charity. That is, we take others as having the same beliefs and desires like our own. Proceeding a step ahead to search for true belief Davidson introduces the notion of Omniscient Interpreter (hereafter OI).[9] This notion states that OI is one who being an interpreter shares most of his beliefs with other speakers and being omniscient his beliefs cannot be wrong. From this analysis it follows that the speaker's beliefs are true since they are concurrent with the beliefs held by OI. This compels Davidson to claim that there must be a separate place for OI in the theory of interpretation.

Now a question may be raised from the standpoint of a sceptic regarding the correctness of beliefs. Responding to this question Davidson says that for a sceptic to doubt the correctness of our belief must satisfy the two following preconditions without which he cannot intelligibly presume his doubt:

a. He/she must share his/her beliefs with us.
b. These beliefs must be largely true.

If a sceptic has to meaningfully doubt the correctness of others' beliefs he has to detect mistake in others' beliefs. This will be possible only through the interpretation of others' beliefs. But for interpretation to be possible the sceptic has to satisfy the above-stated two conditions. He can interpret only if he shares his beliefs with others and if such beliefs are true then as Davidson argues scepticism will be self-defeating.

---

[8] The term "good" expresses the idea that there should not be any bad intentions behind the speaker's utterances.

[9] This term is borrowed from Davidson 1984b: 201.

The nature of belief is not a hypothetical postulation because it interlinks with various behavioural, biological and neurological phenomena as well as various propositional attitudes such as anxiety, hopes and desires. The relationship between beliefs and these elements is so connected that the former cannot be interpreted in isolation from the latter. As a result, beliefs assume a complicated structure which can be grasped only when they are expressed through language. This happens because meaning and belief jointly form a nexus.

According to Davidson, the ability to interpret is central to thinking. This is because thinking is necessary for speaking and for a person having the concept of belief implies that he must be an interpreter and to be an interpreter means he must be a member of a speech community. Further, he says that for a being to have a thought implies that (s)he must have a system of beliefs. The justification for it is that a particular thought is defined only in relation to a system of beliefs within which it has its own place. In this regard, Davidson has given an example which is as follows: "In order to think whether the gun is loaded requires the belief that a gun is a weapon that is a more or less enduring physical object, and so on."[10] These are the beliefs forming a system that "identifies a thought by locating it in a logical and epistemic space".[11]

Through this analysis Davidson ultimately reveals his hidden agenda expressing his faith that beliefs are socially shared and it is only through a common language that we come to know those beliefs. For him, beliefs are not formed in private experiences of the individual nor are there anything called pre-social and pre-linguistic self of the individual. Thus, he defines belief as essentially a social perspective where one can have thoughts only by interpreting the speech of the other. Adding to it, he states that the ability to interpret is the ground for acquiring knowledge; knowledge of how things are in the world.

---

[10] This example is taken from Davidson 1984c: 157.

[11] Ibid.

In this regard, Davidson states that investigation of the nature of thought and investigation of the nature of language are one and the same. But it is noticed that there are differences found between what *X* says and what *X* thinks. Hence, the radical translation is impossible from one language to another because of the improper and inaccurate translation. In this respect, he says that radical interpretation must start from "evidence that can be stated without essential use of such linguistic concepts as meaning, interpretation, synonymy and the like".[12] In case of radical interpretation, he further asserts that to say that "*S* means that *P*" is to say that *S* belongs to a language for which an empirically acceptable calculus of truth conditions delivers "*S* is true iff *P*" as a theorem.[13] Thus, the theorem that leads to the speaker of the language must satisfy the principle of charity.

For Davidson, to determine the meanings of utterances of a speaker we not only hold the charity principle and belief system but also the theory of radical interpretation. These three principles together assist us to understand the speaker's utterances and guide us to relate to the conditions where the sentences will be treated as true or false. Thus, according to Davidson, every sentence can be judged as either true or false. To claim a sentence is true or false depends on its material adequacy condition and formal condition of *T*-sentence. *T*-sentence as such is not free from the problems of determining the meaning of a proposition. The problem lies with *T*-sentence when the object language does not match with the meta-language, i.e. a mismatch between what the sentence expresses and what it refers to. Davidson calls this problem as "extensional problem".

Extensional Problem

An extensionally adequate truth theory yields *T*-sentences which may be regarded as meaning theorems. But the theory which yields

---

[12] This example is taken from Davidson 1984c: 128.

[13] This is enunciated by Hale 2000: 181.

T-sentences of the kind "'snow is white' is true iff grass is green" where the problem arises, since it threatens the very idea of an extensionally adequate truth theory that Davidson seeks to develop.

There are three ways that Davidson has tried to meet this challenge. In Fodor and Lepore's[14] view, these three ways are:

1. The compositionality solution.
2. The nomologicity solution.
3. The charity solution.

The Compositionality Solution

If we carefully notice the procedure through which the *T*-sentences are derived then we will see that the theory in question "must exhibit the semantic properties of the sentence as determined by the semantic properties of its lexical parts together with its syntactic structure".[15] Moreover it is the theory that will arrive at the truth conditions of all the sentences of the language in this way. And it is then alone we can expect that the object language sentence embedded in the *T*-sentence will be correctly interpreted by the matching meta-language sentence. This is definitely a holistic constraint on the truth theory if it has to work as a meaning theory.

The moral is that we can have an extensional theory of meaning as long as we believe that the structural relations between formulas are respected while the derivations of the *T*-sentences are made.

> The fact that each axiom of a truth theory has its impact upon an infinite number of *T*-sentences does indeed have the consequence that it is difficult for counterfeit theories to pass the test.[16]

Now a question arises: is compositionality really required to rule out the possibility of entailment of false sentences? If we are to say that the structural similarity between "snow is white" and "this is snow"

---

[14] These three ideas are found in Fodor and Lepore 1992: 63, 84 and 93.

[15] Ibid.: 63

[16] McDowell and Evans 1976: xv.

is itself enough to ensure the truth of the sentence "'snow is white' is true iff snow is white" then we shall have to say, we have an a priori argument against the possibility of a non-compositional language. Fodor and Lepore have tried to come up with an explanation of such a non-compositional language which as they try to show may have expressions which will have determined truth-conditions.

The Nomologicity Solution

Davidson holds the view that *T*-sentences derived from truth theory are offered as warranted empirical generalizations about the speakers of a language *L* and hence must be not only true but also law like.[17] Here, one may ask if *T*-sentences are law like then can we respect the idea of conventionality of language. Second, *T*-sentences are law like means that they support counterfactuals. What would that mean? It would mean that if we have a *T*-sentence like "Susama is a singer" is true in English iff Susama is a singer, then necessarily in all the possible worlds where "Susama is a singer" is true are the worlds where Susama is a singer. But is there any reason to believe this? There may be a possible world where "Susama is a singer" as a *T*-sentence is true but in actuality its meaning differs from as we understand in English language. It simply means that in possible world the *T*-sentence "Susama is a singer" means "Cow is white".

One answer is that the *T*-sentence in question which says "Susama is a singer" means that *Susama is a singer* in English, and if there is a language where "Susama is a singer" does not mean *Susama is a singer* then that just is not English. But this makes *T*-sentence not nomologically necessary but only conceptually necessary and also it makes the use of the expression in English in the *T*-sentence question begging.

The Charity Solution

Davidson speaks of another constraint on a truth theory if it is to provide us with an interpretation of language which maximizes

---

[17] Fodor and Lepore 1992: 84.

true beliefs. In other words, the truth theory must provide an interpretation which makes most of the sentences held true by the speaker of that language. Succinctly, if we follow a truth theory while interpreting a speaker we should make ascription in a manner that makes most of the beliefs that the speaker holds are true. So, we see that the theory of interpretation has the principle of charity as an essential component as well as holism. As we go about interpreting the speaker, we do it by trying to find out truth conditions of the sentences that (s)he utters only holistically. Here we must not forget that in doing this we have to be radical in our interpretation. By explaining the issue that "when is an interpretation to be radical" Davidson states that radical interpretation is an inferential process which starts with a set of information, all of which is non-semantic, but ends in the attribution of rich and varied meanings.[18]

From the above analysis it is asserted that Davidson's approach to meaning is unique because of his descriptions on "the theory of interpretation" and "the belief system" that in true sense claim to establish his meaning holism. He states that to know the meaning of a sentence means to understand the sentence. And, in order to understand a sentence we need to know the meaning of its constituent words, its usage, the rules through which it governs, and along with those a few further requirements, such as sharedness of belief between the speaker and the hearer, and the theory of radical interpretation. Hence, it is claimed that no sentence could be understood in isolation from other sentences of a given language. Therefore, Davidson's submission is, meaning of an expression is determined in relation to other expressions of a language. Meaning, thus, in the Davidsonian approach works either in a linguistic or in a mental system holistically.

---

[18] Please see Davidson 1984a.

8

Later Wittgenstein and Meaning Holism

After the discussion on Quine's and Davidson's approaches to meaning holism, this chapter is devoted to the discussion on Later Wittgenstein with a view to show how his conception of meaning follows the same track as that of Quine and Davidson. In his *Philosophical Investigations*, Wittgenstein explicitly expresses that to understand the meaning of a proposition we must understand it in relation to other propositions. To establish this claim he has analysed some crucial concepts that are fundamental to meaning. In this respect, the three crucial concepts pertaining to meaning are: use, family resemblance and language-game. All these three concepts advocate Wittgenstein's stand on meaning holism. After reflecting on his prior work the *Tractatus* he feels that there are quite a few problems that need to be discussed further. These problems are recognized and elucidated at the beginning of the *Philosophical Investigations*. While revisiting the *Tractatus* the problems found by Wittgenstein are as follows:

a. The correlation of names with objects.

b. The connection between language and reality.

c. The relation between a proposition and its pictorial form.

The first one states that names have meaning when they stand for some objects or refer to some objects. A name without its referent does not possess any meaning. The bare name for him is just like a sign. The justification he has given is that a sign is nothing but the concatenation of some marks. When a sign conveys some meaning then it is no more a sign. It turns into a symbol. In the same way, a name without meaning is just the connotation of letters. It has meaning when it refers to some objects of the world.

Regarding the connection between language and reality Wittgenstein aptly states that a proposition expresses about the facts of the world. The truth-value of a proposition is determined by the corresponding facts of the world. A proposition will be true only when its corresponding fact is found in the empirical world, otherwise it is treated false.

Concerning the pictorial nature of proposition, Wittgenstein iterates that each proposition depicts a picture. He further adds that complex propositions can be reduced to atomic propositions which are of declarative sort. The picture will decide whether a proposition is true or false. This is because the truth of a proposition is dependent upon the state of affairs that it refers to. This is how the truth of a proposition is determined.

Counteracting the notion that each name refers to the object(s) of the world, Wittgenstein in his later work mentions that there is confusion between the bearer of a name and the meaning of a name (Rhees 1974: 63-64). The following example can clarify this notion. "Gautam Buddha died some years ago." In this sentence, one may claim that since Gautam Buddha, the bearer of the name, died, the name "Gautam Buddha" does not have any meaning. Thus the sentence is meaningless. But this is wrong to claim so. Here, according to Wittgenstein, the bearer of the name dies, but not the meaning of the name. Meaning of the name "Gautam Buddha" remains same today as was earlier. It is no way affected by not having its bearer on the earth. The confusion arises between the bearer and the meaning of a name when a name is explained by pointing to its bearer ostensively. This asserts that to understand a name which is a constituent part of a sentence, we are not only acquainted with its bearer but also able to grasp its role in that sentence, i.e. how it is used. This is how Wittgenstein brings the notion of use as a necessary component of meaning.

Wittgenstein while talking about the connection between language and reality says that every proposition expresses a state of affairs of the world and the truth-value of a sentence is decided on the availability of its corresponding facts in the world. Now the question arises: how do we know which state of affairs the proposition is referring to out of many states of affairs? This is because the world is divided into many facts or states of affairs. This assumes that to know a state of affairs what the proposition is stating about is to know other states of affairs of the world. As a result, we can identify the correct state of affairs that the proposition is stating about. Hence, the truth-value of a proposition is decided. That is how one concept is related to other concepts for its understanding and also how one sentence is related to other sentences for determining its meaning.

Rejecting the view of the pictorial nature of proposition, Wittgenstein conveys that all propositions do not depict the picture. For example, "The eternal truth is ever lasting", "Wow! It is wonderful". A question arises, what sorts of pictures these sentences depict or convey? Here Wittgenstein finds the picture theory of meaning is applicable only to indicative sentences. It cannot be applied to other varieties of sentences of ordinary language. Thus, the theory is too narrow and hence demands revision.

After discussing these problems he tries to come up with a theory for determining the meaning of all sorts of proposition. He states that meaning of a proposition is determined by its use and not by its corresponding state of affairs of the world. Further, he argues that we need not search for the meaning of a proposition, rather we should give our whole attention towards its use, i.e. how words are used in a sentence and how sentences are used in a contextual paradigm of a language. This suggests that meaning of a proposition is derived by looking into its context, i.e. where the proposition is used.

This discussion while expounding Wittgenstein's theory of

meaning holism goes into the details of three notions, namely, "use", "family-resemblance", and "language-game". These three notions are constitutive of Wittgenstein's formulation of meaning as a holistic concept. To start with meaning as use, Wittgenstein expresses that sentences are mere combination of names and function as description. His account on meaning is contributed for understanding a proposition of a language. Here, the analysis is focused upon the constituent word meaning of a sentence and how it is intrinsically related with the explanation of meaning of a sentence. This suggests, "meaning is what is explained in giving an explanation of meaning" (*PG*: 68f).[1]

Wittgenstein's approach to meaning suggests the idea that meaning functions holistically in a language. This view is found in the later part of his work expressed in various forms, such as "meaning of a word is its use in a language", "meaning of a word is its use in a calculus" and "meaning of a word is its use in a language-game" (*PG*: 60, 63, 67). He says that in order to grasp the meaning of a word we should not look for an object for which it stands but study the diversity of its functions. In this connection, he announces that the theory of meaning establishes parity between the meaning of a proposition, the understanding of a proposition and the explanation of a proposition. It is a relationship where one follows from the other. Meaning is ultimately thus what is given by explanation of meaning.

On Wittgenstein's account, propositions are descriptions of facts and there exists an internal relation between the use of propositions and the determination of meanings of propositions. "Meaning" and "use" are thus inextricable notions. As he argues, all words are names. We explain a word by means of a sentence of the form "'X signifies . . .', so we can explain any sentence by means of a sentence of the form *P* describes the fact that . . ." (Baker and Hacker 1983: 60). He thus concludes that every sentence

[1] PG stands for the text "Philosophical Grammar". For detail, see Rhees 1974.

is essentially a description. The analysis or the description of a sentence is indispensable for revealing its form.

There are two ways of analysing a sentence:

First, there are possibilities where we can translate a sentence into an equivalent sentence possessing the same use and the same form through which the description is given. For example, the analysis of a sentence "Is it the case that *P*?" might be translated into "I would like to know whether it is the case that *P*" (*Philosophical Investigations* (*PI*) # 24). In the similar way, the translation procedure can be applied to all other forms of sentences.

Second, analysis brings out from every sentence its use. It reveals a crucial fact that a sentence with different uses may have an identical descriptive content. It assumes that understanding the context of a sentence where it is used gives a complete understanding of its meaning. Hence it is viewed that the essential feature of a sentence is its description. In this regard Wittgenstein says, "look at the sentence as an instrument, and at its sense as its employment" (*PI* #421). The meaning of a sentence thus according to him is essentially related to the criterion of understanding.

Wittgenstein says, understanding a word is a matter of knowing how to use it correctly, i.e. of having mastery of its use. In a similar fashion, understanding a sentence seems a matter of having mastery of its use and using it correctly is a criterion of understanding it. Hence, understanding an utterance implies mastery of the practice in which a sentence is used as an instrument. From this, it is understood that meaning is context specific. To determine the meaning of a proposition we see in what context it is used. To identify a context means to know how it differs from other contexts. So, we acquire the knowledge of other contexts. Hence, we know where the sentence is to be applied. This conveys the idea that determination of meaning of a proposition depends on the understanding of its context, i.e. how a particular proposition expresses a specific meaning when it is used in a particular context and changes its meaning while used in other contexts. Thus, meaning of a proposition is determined in relation to other propositions of a language. This amounts to the holistic approach to meaning.

In this regard, Wittgenstein asserts that in order to understand a sentence we need to understand other sentences of a particular language. On his view, understanding is an ability, more accurately, understanding is akin to an ability. Thus, a person who understands something is able to do certain things. For example, a person who understands a sentence of his/her native language can do many things, e.g. paraphrase it, explain it at length, use it in appropriate contexts, respond to it in appropriate ways (Baker and Hacker 1983: 344). This proclaims that understanding is a family resemblance concept.

The criterion for understanding a sentence is of two sorts.

a. To give a correct explanation.

b. Using the expression correctly.

Sentences are the fundamental units of "speech" and regarded as the basic ingredient of language. In this connection, it may be stated that someone who understands the meaning of a word can explain it correctly and can use it correctly in sentences. In a similar fashion, if a person understands a sentence it implies that (s)he is aware of its use and its correct interpretation.

From this analysis it is derived that:

i. All sentences are the descriptions of facts.

ii. There is an inherence relation exists between use of sentences and the determination of meanings of sentences.

The first one states that every sentence describes a fact of the world. Thus, to understand a sentence means to know the state of affairs the sentence is stating about. Recognizing and identifying the state of affairs acquire the ability to discriminate it from other state of affairs of the world. Hence, to know a state of affairs means to be aware of other states of affairs that are either similar or dissimilar with it. Thus, understanding a sentence requires understanding of other sentences. Hence, meaning works holistically.

The second one is about the intrinsic relation between the determination of meaning of sentences and the use of those sentences. This states that correct use of a sentence results into the proper understanding of that sentence. Again, understanding a sentence requires understanding of other sentences. Thus, to know how to use a sentence in a particular context means to know its meaning, and therefore, knowing the meanings of other related (interconnected) sentences. Hence, meaning is not determined in isolation from other sentences. Thus, understanding a sentence requires understanding of other sentences. Hence, Wittgenstein's approach to meaning is considered to be holistic in nature.

The relation between explanation of meaning of an expression and understanding of that expression is an internal one. It is so because if a person understands the explanation of *X*, then (s)he understands *X*. This is a general feature of understanding a language, namely, that explanation is internally related to meaning and understanding. Thus, it is stated that a criterion for my not understanding a grammatical explanation of *X* implies I do not use *X* correctly. From this, it is asserted that "understanding" is a family resemblance term, naming a family of process (*PG:* 74). Thus, Wittgenstein holds the view that understanding consists of "a whole bundle of processes, dispositions, experiences, patterns of behaviour which are bounded together by language into a sort of unity".[2]

Under the following heading we shall discuss the importance and intricacy of the concept "family resemblance" and show how it supports the theory of meaning holism. In addition to these, how Wittgenstein argues about a group of sentences as a whole function for determining the meaning of a sentence, and in what ways a

---

[2] This sentence is borrowed from Waismann 1965: 348.

bunch of or a set of sentences is regarded as a family sentence will be our consideration for discussions.

Family Resemblance

The notion "family resemblance" is mostly associated with Wittgenstein's conception of language-game. The *locus classicus* of the elucidation of the notion family resemblance is found in the *Philosophical Investigations* (*PI* # 65-71). This notion is introduced and clarified primarily with reference to the concept of game. The following discussions will elucidate how "family resemblance" is understood with reference to the analysis of the concept of "game".

The concept of game is closely connected with the theory of meaning as use. According to Wittgenstein, meaning of a word is the role that plays in the calculus of a sentence. This he says by comparing a chess piece in the game of chess, i.e. how a chess piece moves in the chess-game. The term "game" according to Wittgenstein is a family-likeness term (*PG*: 75). He says that the feature of game can share with language-game. Even though not all games have similar rules, the function of rules in many games has similarities. It is like the function of rules in a language. Thus, the function of language can be regarded as "language-game". The study of language-game is the study of primitive forms of language or primitive language.

The concept of meaning may be described with a primitive idea of the way language functions. In this regard Wittgenstein gives an example of an assistant and how he understands his master's words in constructing a building. There is a prior understanding between the assistant and the master which helps the assistant to understand what his master says:

> Let us imagine a language which serves the purpose for the communication between a builder *A* and his helper *B* to construct a building. *A* is building with building stones: there are blocks, pillars, slabs and beams. *B* has to pass the stones, and that in the order in which *A* needs them. For this purpose they use a language

> consisting of the words "block", "pillar", "slab", "beam". *A* calls them out; — *B* brings the stone which he has learnt to bring at such-and-such a call conceive this as a complete primitive language. — Schulte 2004: 26

While analysing the language-game, Wittgenstein says that a proposition is the basic unit of a language. To understand the meaning of a proposition, it is not just enough to know the meanings of the constituent words, but we must know their special contributions to the sentence and the context where the sentence is used. Thus understanding a proposition presupposes understanding of other propositions. This indicates that meaning works holistically.

On the account of Wittgenstein, "primitive language" and "language-game" are interchangeable, which he admits in *Philosophical Investigations* # 7: "Sometimes speak of a primitive language as a language-game". Further, he says "to imagine a primitive language — language game means to imagine a form of life" (*PI* # 19). Here he does not mean that to imagine a language like French means to imagine a form of life in the sense of the French way of life. Rather, he means that it is to imagine a primitive language — language-game like that of the builders. The form of life involved in imagining a primitive language will have to be a form of our life; that is a human form of life.

Thus to understand a sentence we need to know not only its meaning, but also how it differs from other sentences and in which context it is used. This is precisely called "language-game" by Wittgenstein. By adapting this process a child learns language. A child learns the meaning of a word by the help of its referent and discriminating it from its non-referents.

Language-game is referring to the linguistic practices and the formulation of criterion that we found while understanding a sentence in a contextual paradigm of a language. It is the platform where we find a link between language and reality. Elaborating this view Wittgenstein in his *Philosophical Investigations* says that meaning cannot be acquired just by observing the expressions of a language and their relation to the worldly affairs. Nor can they be read off from the mental contents of the language users. So, we need a "primitive language-game" for understanding an utterance of a speaker. A "primitive language-game" may be defined as "a pattern of behaviour in which one participant responds to a signal or communication by doing something directly observable and immediately intelligible" (" 1986: 76). Primitive language helps to identify the context in which the speaker is conversing language and thereby we understand the meaning of speaker's utterances.

Speaking of language is part of a communal activity. It is through participating in the common language-game that language is connected with our life (*PG*: 65). In this connection Wittgenstein enunciates that language-game encompasses the notion "form-of-life". This is because language communicates in a community-based society. In a society though we find the different patterns of behaviour among the individuals yet there is an underlying unity is found among these behavioural differences. The underlying unity is the understanding of one another's language. This understanding is possible because of the uniformity that is found in the community. Wittgenstein calls this the "form-of-life" within which individuals in a community participate. The concept of "form-of-life" is similar to the concept of "family resemblance". The reason is that each individual in a family although behaves differently, we find certain commonality among the members of a family.

Now a question arises: what is the role of "language-game" that helps to understand the speaker's utterances? Wittgenstein responds to this query in the light of his analysis of the game of chess.

Chess Analogy

Wittgenstein states that a game of chess is not about the chess pieces but it is about the meaning of a chess piece which is associated by the sum of rules that determines its possible movements. In a similar way, a sentence of a language has a specific meaning by virtue of its contribution of constituent word meaning, their usage and the rules that govern the sentence. On his view, the chess analogy can usefully illuminate the features of logical syntax of a language. If language is conceived as a logico-syntactical calculus, then chess analogy can bring to the light the following features:

i. Like the rules of chess the rules of language have no foundations and cannot be justified by reference to reality. Its rules are autonomous; nothing dictates them.

ii. Its rules are arbitrary and could be different; change the rules and you change the game.

iii. The logical syntax of a word determines its place in grammar and in this sense is akin to the rules determining the possible moves of a chess piece.

iv. All that is lacking is the assignment of meaning, i.e. a method of application. It is the method of application that differentiates language (and applied mathematics) from chess (and pure mathematics) (Baker and Hacker 1983: 48-49).

Again, by comparing language-game with chess, he says:[3]

a. The outward similarity of words is comparable to that of chess pieces, and is no less misleading (*PG*: 59).

b. The combinatorial possibilities of words are comparable to the possible configuration of chess pieces.

c. The use of a word in an utterance is like the use of chess piece in a move.

d. The meaning of a word is (up to a point) analogous to the powers of a chess piece.

e. Just as a chess piece has significance only in the context of a move in a game so a word has a meaning only in the context of a sentence and a sentence has meaning only in a language.

---

[3] The following point sare borrowed from Baker and Hacker 1983: 49.

f. Understanding a word is not a mental state, event or process, but an ability to use it in certain ways for certain purposes, just as knowing how to play chess is knowing how to move the pieces in conformity with the rules of chess in pursuit of the goal of winning — in both cases a technique is mastered (*Manuscripts* 166, vol. II: 28F).[4]

Wittgenstein attacks the calculus model of language but holds the chess analogy as useful medium to explain the determination of meaning of a proposition. In this regard, it may be pointed out that he rejects the reductionist's view by stating that a proposition won't be reduced to either a set of propositions or to an atomic proposition which is conclusively verifiable by reference to what is immediately given in experience. This suggests that he rejects the foundationalism in epistemology. His way of explaining the foundationalism revolves around the socialized epistemology instead of naturalized epistemology. On this account, he agrees that language learning rests upon training and further, language acquisition presupposes neither thought nor innate knowledge. On his view, language learning is a heuristic device to illuminate the concepts of language, meaning and understanding. Hence, "the common behaviour of mankind is the system of reference by means of which we interpret an unknown language" (*PI* # 206).

In the context of language-game Wittgenstein says that a sentence in general is the minimal unit by which a move is made in the language-game. It is only with sentences that we actually say something. He further insists that understanding a sentence implies knowing what it expresses, and understanding begins with the whole sentence (*PG* # 44). The use of a sentence is akin to the move of a chess piece and a move is only a move in the context of a game. So, a sentence has no meaning in isolation. Understanding a language is the background against which a sentence acquires meaning as understanding chess is for moving chess pieces. So,

[4] L. Wittgenstein, 1929-1944, *Manuscripts*, vol. II. For more detail see Baker and Hacker 2009.

a sentence acquires meaning in the "game of language". Hence, to understand a sentence is to understand a language (*Blue and Brown Books* # 5; *PI* # 199). Here Wittgenstein is not committed to the absurd view that one cannot understand any part of language unless one understands every part. For him, language must be segmentable otherwise neither learning nor teaching would be possible. In this regard, it is stated that understanding a sentence requires understanding of other sentences in a particular paradigm of a given language.

According to Wittgenstein, understanding a fact or a proposition depends upon the speaker's behaviour. He writes:

> I conceive of understanding, in a sense, behaviouristically. . . what is behaviourist in my conception consists only in that I do not distinguish between "outer" and "inner", because psychology does not concern me. — *The Big Typescript* 284

His dictum is, understanding a sentence means understanding a few other sentences of a language. He also subscribes to the notion "web of belief" by which he means all statements are inherently constituted with beliefs and all beliefs are differently related to experiences. Out of those beliefs some exposed to direct verification and some are resulted in falsification. Hence, "all testing, all confirmation and disconfirmation of a proposition takes place within a system. The system is the element in which arguments have their life" (*OC*/von Wright, Anscombe, and Paul 1969: 105).

Wittgenstein further conveys "use" of an expression signifies not merely behaviour but rule-governed behaviour or more generally, behaviour subject to standards of correctness. It is like the use of a chess piece in a game. The chess piece is not merely the way in which people move it but the way they move it and when they move it correctly — it is in accordance with the rules for its use. Hence, language learning is indeed rooted in training, and such training is in some ways similar to setting up a causal mechanism by stimulus conditioning. From this, it does not follow that in general "the pronouncement of a word is now a stimulus, now a reaction" (*PLP*/Waismann and Harre 1965: 113).

Wittgenstein argues that to use a sentence correctly is not a statistical concept.[5] Use of an expression is not just the verbal behaviours of the users, rather it is the mixture of verbal behaviours along with other behaviours in so far as it accords with the acknowledged rules for the correct employment of that expression. Users themselves acknowledge these rules in their humdrum explanation of meaning. It is the explanation of meaning that constitutes standards for the correct use of their explananda and what counts as a correct application of an expression is exhibited in the practice of its application. In this connection, Wittgenstein argues that communication takes place between the hearer and the speaker when there will be an either agreement or disagreement in their judgements. In case of disagreement, the speaker communicates his view to the hearer but their disagreement might be due to various reasons, such as, illogical arguments, ideology-based reasons, and many more. Not only that but also in terms of definitions or explanations of meaning in standards of correct use. Hence, we find an internal and inherence relation between explanation of meaning of an expression and application of that expression. From this it is asserted that meaning of an expression is determined by its use. It is given by what are accepted as explanations of meaning. It is what we understood when we understand what an expression means. And that is exhibited in the criterion of understanding. Expressions are synonymous if their explanations refer to the same object or a particular fact or serve the same purposes.

From this, it is enunciated that Wittgensteinian approach to meaning holism subscribes to the radical interpretation in behaviouristic fashion. His behaviouristic approach to radical interpretation may be explained as "understanding" occurs in a

[5] Baker and Hacker 1983: 12.

mental state and it is akin to the capability of an individual hence it is ascertained that the nature of capacity and the degree to which it is processed are to be seen in an individual's behaviour including his/her linguistic behaviour. In this connection, Wittgenstein speaks about the "common behaviour of mankind" in reference to the interpretation of unknown languages and the languages that are conceived intentionally. It will be much clearer if we give an example in this regard. An explorer when he comes to a foreign land can come to know (understand) the native language and this is possible when he comes in close contact with the natives; in a sense, he participates in their form of life.

To understand an unknown language or a conceptual scheme, we have to determine its ontological imports and try to translate it into another language. Translating or interpreting a sentence needs ability of a person but understanding a sentence demands one must engage in it. Thus, it is viewed that "speaking a language is part of form of life" (*Manuscripts* 119, vol. I).

Wittgenstein's analysis of understanding a sentence relates with explanation and manifestation of its correct application where the correct application is internally related to the explanation. In his view, sentences are the minimal units of interpreting a language and hence moving towards language-game. Therefore, use of sentences in a language is embedded in the stream of human life. It is a part of the endlessly differentiated pattern of human behaviour. In this connection he states that to understand a sentence means to understand a language.

According to Wittgenstein, as Quine puts it, "language is social in essence. It is a social art, socially inculcated which we all acquire on the evidence solely of other peoples' overt behaviour under publicly recognizable circumstances" (Quine 1981: 192; *PPI*/Quine 1969: 26-27). Parallel to Wittgenstein's view, Quine also suggests that "language is a skill that each of us acquires from his/her fellows through mutual observation, emulation, and correction in jointly observable circumstances. When we learn the meaning of an expression we learn only what is observable in overt verbal behaviour and its circumstances" (Quine 1987a: 130; Arrington and Glock 1996: 120).

For Wittgenstein, use of a word is its function in the language-game (*PI* # 21). "One cannot guess how a word functions. One has to look at its use and learn from that" (*PI* # 340). One way of observing "use" is to follow his/her often given advice and considers how a child might learn a given piece of language. What he means is that learning can take place or meaning of a proposition could be determined if we see the context in which a sentence is used and the employment of words that are used in a sentence. The "context" is internally connected to the "use". Hence, it is asserted that the different contexts correspond to their multiple uses.

To utter a word in a given context is to engage in a language-game. Language-games are customs (*PI* # 199). In learning to speak, the child articulates his thoughts which means he acquires one by one a mastery of the customs that make up language. In this context Wittgenstein states that "the common behaviour of mankind is the system of reference by means of which we interpret an unknown language" (*PI* # 206).

Wittgenstein: The Common Behaviour of Mankind and Forms of Life

By handling the problem of radical interpretation Wittgenstein says that we share with the natives certain basic forms of human behaviour.[6] This idea is linked with the claim that "speaking a language is part of a form of life", i.e. a communal practice in which our language-games are embedded (*PI* # 23; *RFM*/von Wright, Rhees and Anscombe 1978: 335). He says that what allows us to translate an alien language is the fact that we share with speakers' "common form of life", namely "human form of life". It is also called "human facts of life". The reason is Wittgenstein sometimes calls "forms of life", "facts of life". This is because he includes human behaviours

[6] Arrington and Glock 1996: 165.

within it specifically as the sum total of communal activities. Often he speaks "forms of life" in plural (*RPPI*/von Wright and Nyman 1980: 630; *CE*/Rhees 1976: 404). In his view, it is reasonable to assume that "forms of life" do not refer to our common biological nature but to our culture and social transformations which are shared among us.

Wittgenstein also insists that there are minimum requirements that a form of linguistic behaviour must meet in order to be intelligible. This is also echoed in the writings of Quine and Davidson. So, his claim is, we could never start the hermeneutical process unless we shared with the interpreters' certain forms of life or facts of life (*RFM*/von Wright, Rhees and Anscombe 1978: 414, 421). Adding to this point he further says unless the natives shared their desire to communicate with the linguist, the mutual instruction (i.e. querying and correction) between the linguist and natives would not take place. Thus he writes that translating words from an alien language to other languages which are in the forms of doubt, certainly lies mainly on gestures and the facial expressions of the speakers and their tone of voices (*Early Big Typescript* 1932: 149). It is a matter of empirical fact that some features of human behaviour concerning gestures, facial expressions, demeanour and intonation have trans-cultural significance.[7] Thus, he speaks that radical translation requires a substantial overlap with forms of life.

He eloquently expresses that "if language is to be a means of communication there must be agreement and disagreement not only in definitions but also . . . in judgements" (*PI* # 242). To understand what people says we need to judge whether they are speaking the truth or not. Hence, "sharing a language is not agreement in opinions but in forms of life" (*PI* # 241). From this analysis it is asserted that understanding an alien language presumes not only convergence of beliefs but also a pattern of behaviour, which in turn presupposes a framework of shared cognitive capacities, needs, emotions and attitudes (Arrignton and Glock 1996: 169).

---

[7] Please see Izard 1969.

From the above analysis it is asserted that Wittgenstein's approach to meaning is a holistic one. His discussion shows that meaning of a sentence is derived from the network of sentences. To derive meaning from the web of sentences or network of sentences is to observe an essential feature identified as intraconnection of sentences in a language. In this regard, he argues that to determine the meaning of a sentence we require a few more sentences which are related to that sentence either directly or indirectly, or inferentially. Hence, to understand a sentence we need to understand the language as a whole by which it is constituted of. This assumes that understanding a concept or a fact deals with our forms of life. His explanation of forms of life includes network of beliefs, patterns of behaviour, customs and culture of a society and in general, socialized life. Hence his submission is, to understand a fact which is represented by a sentence ascribes the holistic theory. That is to determine the meaning of a sentence we need a group of sentences within a particular paradigm of a language. This shows that meaning is embedded in the language in a holistic way.

9

Conclusion

Towards an Idea of a Moderate Meaning Holism

To support the theory meaning holism is to accept the argument that meaning of a proposition is determined in relation to other propositions of a given language. This view is suggested by Quine, Davidson and Later Wittgenstein in their own way which we have discussed elaborately. Their view on holism is a global one. The phrase "global holism" as Dummett used it (which he criticized) is expressed differently by Davidson as "full-blooded holism" and by Quine as "corporate holism". They state that to understand a proposition the interpreter must be aware of other propositions so that (s)he can differentiate the meaning of the given proposition from other propositions. In this process the interpreter knows what the proposition is stating about, what it refers to and how it differs from other propositions. This is the way how the interpreter knows the meaning of all other propositions.

This view is challenged by Dummett. He claims that meaning holism is acceptable but not the kind of holism that is proposed by Quine and Davidson. On his view, meaning holism as a theory can be of different kinds such as global holism, moderate holism and molecular holism.

The "moderate holism" which is acceptable to Dummett is also termed as "sophisticated holism". He rejects both "global holism" and "molecular holism".

Dummett's Refutation of Global Holism

Davidson and Quine hold the view that to understand the meaning of a sentence we require other sentences of that particular language. This implies to determine the meaning of a proposition we need to determine the meaning of other propositions of that language. This asserts that meaning works holistically in a global fashion. This view is refuted by Dummett. He raises a question regarding global holistic conception of meaning. That is, how is it possible that to understand the meaning of a sentence we require to understand all the sentences of that language? He further points out that if it is so then how a language can be learnt? Again, to understand all the sentences, we have to start somewhere, i.e. from a particular sentence. If our understanding starts with a particular sentence then how can we argue that we understand all the sentences of that language simultaneously? Hence, the theory of global holism is not tenable for determining the meaning of a proposition. Dummett in this context says that learning is always piecemeal, i.e. we learn sentences one after another, but we do not learn language as a whole.

Dummett while arguing against the Davidsonian theory of meaning says that Davidson has not provided an account in his truth theory which can explicate the semantics in terms of non-semantics. What he means is that, Davidson explains the truth theory, i.e. to determine the meaning of a sentence we need to know the exact state of affairs what it refers to. But the question arises, how is it that we can refer to the exact state of affairs without knowing other state of affairs of the world? Elaborating it further Dummett argues how does a person know snow is white in the empirical world without knowing how snow differs from or similar like other objects? Thus, Davidsonean arguments for determining the meaning of a proposition end up with logical difficulties.

According to Davidson, meaning and truth-value are interconnected. One cannot be separated from the other. In this context, it is stated that a proposition is meaningful while it has truth-value and inversely, a proposition has truth-value means it possesses a specific meaning. Objecting this view, Dummett argues there can be a possibility of meaning determination without determining the truth-value. Consider the sentence "X behaves wrongly". The meaning of this sentence is determined by observing his/her actions. The action performed by X is to be regarded as non-semantic which in turn determines the semantics of the sentence. The meaning of the sentence is thus determined by observing the action done by X and not by analysing the meaning of the expression "wrong". This perspective on meaning (i.e. defining semantics in terms of non-semantics) is not found in Davidson's approach to meaning.

Dummett argues that Davidson does not satisfy the principle of manifestability when he explains the theory of meaning in terms of the theory of truth which is an extension of Tarski's truth theory. Dummett's worry is, can't there be a theory of truth which is understood as same as a theory of meaning? If not, then we lead to a vicious circle of infinite regress. The infinite regress involved here is that either the meaning of a proposition is determined by its truth-value or the truth-value of a proposition is decided by considering the meaning of a proposition. Thus Dummett says that to avoid the infinite regress we must accept the principle of manifestability which conveys that the truth-value of a proposition can be determined by the meaning of the given proposition.

Dummett's Criticism on Quinean Holism

Quine's version of meaning holism states that to understand or to know the meaning of a sentence we require to know the meanings of all the sentences of a given language. In his words, our statements about the external world face the tribunal of sense experience not individually but only as a corporate body (*TDE*: 92).[1] He argues

[1] TDE stands for *Two Dogmas of Empiricism*. For detail, please see Quine 1961.

that determination of the meaning of a sentence deals with the empirical evidences. So the confirmation or disconfirmation of the meaning of a sentence depends on the empirical evidences. Hence, the meaning of a sentence is the method of empirically confirming or infirming it.

Dummett questions Quine's view by arguing that how is it possible to acquire meaning of all the possible sentences of a language without having the meaning of an individual sentence? Again, how is it viable that one must first understand the meaning of all the sentences of a language in order to understand meaning of a particular sentence? For Quine, the interconnection between the sentences among a group and the connection between a group of sentences with the group of observable experiences implies the holistic nature of meaning. Here Quine says that meaning works holistically in the natural language yet it is not free from problems. The difficulty lies if the meaning of a sentence in a group becomes problematic (i.e. either it is semantically anomalous or syntactically ill-formed), it affects the whole body including the related observable experiences. But as he says, due to this threat we cannot claim that the theory goes wrong. What we have to do is to find out which sentence creates problem. Hence, we can modify the sentence or we may replace the sentence. Thus, the theory never goes wrong if one of its premises goes wrong. In this regard, Dummett says that true, affecting the meaning of a sentence affects the other sentences in a group and hence, it disturbs the group of observable sense-experiences. Dummett further points out against Quine that once the whole system gets disturbed it is very difficult to find out which sentence is the root cause for all these disturbances. Since everything gets disturbed, the theory collapses. It does not await a while. Hence, to hold the theory further serves no purpose. The following diagram is constructed here to explain Dummett's stand.

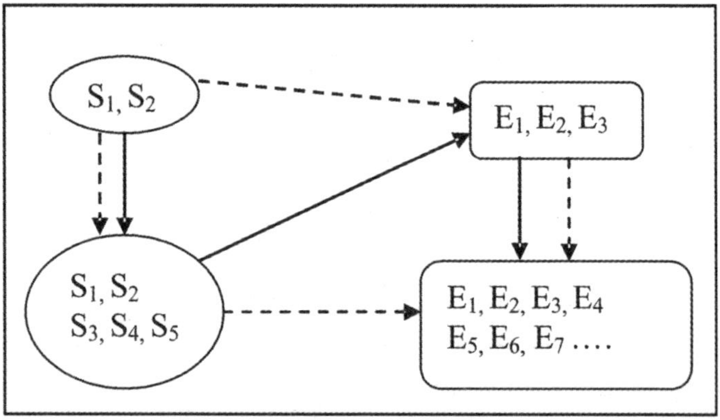

S = Sentence; *E* = Sense experience

Meaning holism collapse

Dummett claims that meaning of a sentence can be changed as per as our experience. For example, a baby understands a sentence "Fire burns" as "fire is hot". When he becomes an adult he understands the sentence as he understood in his childhood. But his adult understanding adds something more to it. He understands meaning of the sentence differently when it is uttered in a different context, where two friends are quarrelling with each other over an issue. Seeing their fight an outsider utters the sentence "Fire burns". In this case, the meaning of the sentence is not same as the meaning that he had learnt in his childhood. In view of these differences in the meaning of the same sentence the question arises, how does Quine's theory of meaning holism can be sustained?

It is practically impossible to hold the Quinean holistic approach to meaning because of the high degree of complexity found in his theory. The complexity arises due to the complicated nature of interconnection existing among sentences. Further, a group or a set of sentences has been defined as the primary unit of meaning.

According to Dummett, a theory of meaning would be judged as correct if we derive the actual correlation between the following two boxes as indicated in the diagram below.

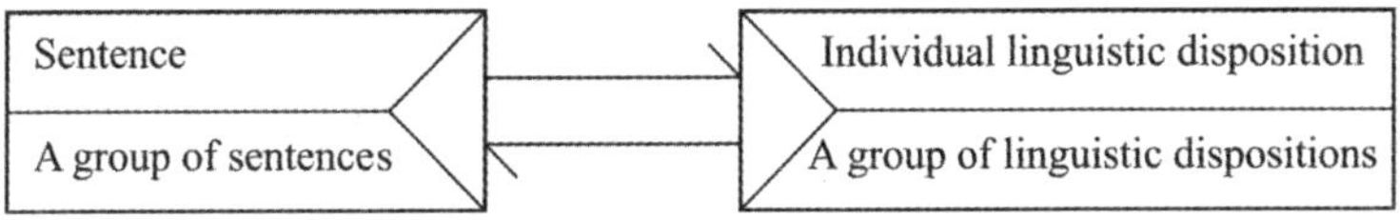

Thus for him, the theory gets confirmation by the observation of linguistic expressions.

Dummett argues that Quinean holistic picture of meaning is a complex and a complicated one, because we not only have to map between the group of expressions and the group of observable sensory experiences but more to it we have to make an internal mapping between individual sentences within a group. As we have stated that meaning of an expression can be changed as per our experience. In this process the mapping between an expression with the further expression may be changed. Here, Dummett says Quine is certainly wrong when he says in a holistic nature of meaning, the individual sentence has no meaning.

The following diagram shows the complication of Quinean version of meaning holism.

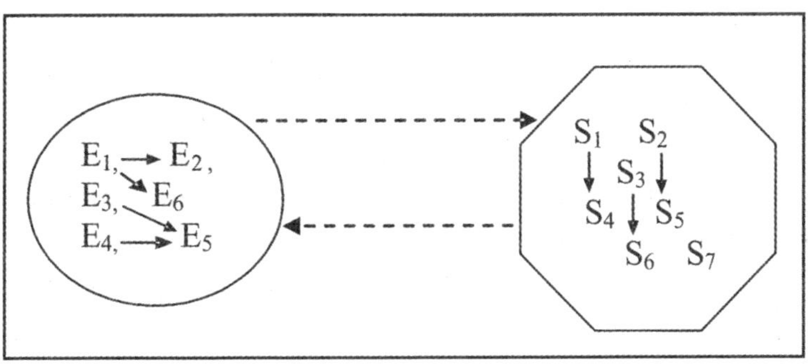

E = Expression; *S* = Sense experience

The complication of Quinean meaning holism

Problems of Molecular Holism

The phrase "molecular holism" gives the impression that it is a "contradiction in terms" but it is not so. It is a fact that can be analysed within the framework of meaning holism. The notion "molecular holism" claims that to understand a proposition we invariably need to understand the specified propositions which are marked forever without any variations or subject to change. Hence, we find a serious problem, i.e. how to determine what are the sentences required for understanding a proposition? In other words, how to delimit the scope for understanding a proposition? Again, how to demarcate the limit and specify the boundary for determining the meaning of a proposition?

If we attempt to demarcate the limit or put a boundary for determining meaning of a proposition then we have to do the same for all the propositions of a language. Such an exercise needless to say is pointless. This is so because different variations of concatenation of terms in ordinary language create *n*-number of sentences. As a result, specifying the boundary of each sentence for determining their meaning will turn out to be a useless affair. Moreover, there is every possibility that delimiting the boundary for determining the meaning of a proposition will result in overlapping of the propositions. In view of these difficulties molecular holism too cannot be sustained.

Another problem pops up, "Is it possible for us to gather all the possible propositions of ordinary language?" A simple answer may be given for this query. That is, ordinary language is so vast that it stretches to an open ended. From this endless corpus how can anyone carry out the above task successfully?

If we cannot gather all the sentences of the ordinary language, how can we understand a sentence? It shows that molecular holism is a weaker version of meaning holism and it cannot account for the defining feature of meaning holism.

Dummett's Submission for Meaning Holism

After rebuking "global holism" theory on one hand and "molecular holism" theory on the other hand, Dummett has given his own version of meaning holism which he characterizes as "moderate holism" or "sophisticated holism". In this context, he explicitly expresses that to determine the meaning of a proposition we require some propositions; but not necessarily all the possible propositions of a language. According to him, an expression for its understanding requires some propositions within a particular paradigm of a language.

He further says, we can have the function between the group of sentences and the observable sense-experiences but not necessarily this will be an instance of one-to-one mapping relation between them. Thus, he accepts that an individual sentence has a specific meaning within the group of sentences.

Dummett accepts the view that understanding a proposition requires other propositions which involves thought processes. To operationalize this view he introduced "content holism", where he elucidates how mental processes are involved with thought and how each thought is embedded in the specific proposition to express the meaning of the proposition. He further points out that a single thought is not involved for understanding a proposition. It is a network of thoughts which are involved for understanding a proposition. In other words, a bunch of thoughts forms the preconditions for understanding the meaning of a proposition. Thus, understanding a proposition involves in a holistic approach to meaning.

Dummett says, to subscribe moderate holism we must take two components into our consideration. These are:

i. Availability of information.

ii. Rational intelligence.

Though these two components vary from person to person and situation to situation, the common theme that remains invariant is to understand a sentence we need a bunch of sentences in a particular paradigm of a given language. For example, let us consider two persons belong to two different places. One is from a remote rural area and another is from a cosmopolitan city. Both of them understand the expression "strawberry" differently on the basis of their geographical, educational and cultural backgrounds. But the fact remains that the term "strawberry" for both of them mean that it is a fruit and it is eatable. Here, though their understanding of the term "strawberry" differs they can share with each other what strawberry means. This is possible due to the holistic nature of meaning.

On the basis of the present discussions, we would now like to submit a view on meaning. Meaning certainly works holistically but holism that is assured here is moderate holism and not global holism. Moderate meaning holism claims that in order to understand meaning of a proposition we do not need to consider the entire body of propositions of a language but only a few to be considered either directly or inferentially that will fulfil the semantic need.

Bibliography

Abelson, R., 1957, "Meaning, Use and Rules of Use", *Philosophy and Phenomenological Research*, 18(1): 48-58.

Achinstein, P., 1964, "On the Meaning of Scientific Terms", *The Journal of Philosophy*, 61(17): 497-509.

Aldrich, V.C., 1936, "A Note on the Empirical Meaning of 'Possible'", *Analysis*, 4(1): 12-14.

——, 1940, "The Spirit of the New Positivism", *Journal of Philosophy*, 37(16): 431-37.

Alston, W.P., 1963, "The Quest for Meaning", *Mind*, 72(285): 79-87.

Ambrose, A. (ed.), 1979, *Wittgenstein's Lectures: Cambridge, 1932-1935*, Oxford: Basil Blackwell.

Ammereller, E. and E. Fischer (eds.), 2004, *Wittgenstein at Work: Methods in the Philosophical Investigation*, New York: Routledge.

Ammerman, R.R., 1965, *Classics of Analytic Philosophy*, Bombay: Tata McGraw-Hill.

Anscombe, G.E.M., 1971, *An Introduction to Wittgenstein's Tractatus*, London: Hutchinson University Library.

Anscombe, G.E.M and P. Geach, 1973, *Three Philosophers*, Oxford: Basil Blackwell.

Arrington, R.L. and H. Glock (eds.), 1996, *Wittgenstein and Quine*, New York: Routledge.

Ayer, A.J., 1933, "Atomic Propositions", *Analysis*, 1(1): 2-6.

——, 1935, "The Criterion of Truth", *Analysis*, 3(1/2): 28-32.

——, 1936, "The Principle of Verifiability", *Mind*, 45(178): 199-203.

——, 1940, *The Foundations of Empirical Knowledge*, London: Macmillan.

——, 1954, "Statements about the Past", *Philosophical Essays*, London: Macmillan.

——, (ed.), 1959, *Logical Positivism*, London: Allen & Unwin.

——, 1976, *Language, Truth and Logic*, London: Penguin.

——, 1985, *Ludwing Wittgenstein*, England: Penguin Books.

Baker, G.P. and P.M.S. Hacker, 1980, *Wittgenstein: Understanding and Meaning: An Analytical Commentary on the Philosophical Investigations*, Oxford: Basil Blackwell.

——, 1983, *Wittgenstein: Meaning and Understanding, Essays on Philosophical Investigation*, vol. 1, Oxford: Basil Blackwell.

——, 2009, *Wittgenstein: Rules, Grammar and Necessity, Essays and Exegesis of §§ 185-242*, vol. 2, UK: Wiley Blackwell.

Baldwin, T., 1991, "The Identity Theory of Truth", *Mind*, 100: 35-51.

Basson, A.H., 1948-49, "Logic and Fact", *Analysis*, 8(6): 81-87.

Baylis, C.A., 1936, "Are Some Propositions Neither True Nor False?", *Philosophy of Science*, 3(2): 156-66.

Becker, K., 1998, "On the Perfectly General Nature of Instability in Meaning Holism", *Journal of Philosophy*, 95: 635-40.

Bell, David, 1979, *Frege's Theory of Judgment*, Oxford: Clarendon Press.

Bell, D., 1987a, "Thoughts", *Notre Dame Journal of Formal Logic*, 28: 36-50.

——, 1987b, "The Art of Judgment", *Mind*, 96: 221-24.

——, 1996, "The Formation of Concepts and the Structure of Thoughts", *Philosophy and Phenomenological Research*, 56: 583-96.

Benjamin, A.C., 1936 "Outlines of an Empirical Theory of Meaning", *Philosophy of Science*, 3(3): 250-66.

——, 1941, "Is Empiricism Self-Refuting?", *Journal of Philosophy*, 38(21): 568-73.

——, 1943, "The Essential Problem of Empiricism", *Philosophy of Science*, 10(1): 13-17

Bergmann, G., 1954, *The Metaphysics of Logical Positivism*, London: Longmans.

Berlin, I., 1968, "Verification", in *The Theory of Meaning*, ed. G.H.R. Parkinson, Oxford: Oxford University Press.

Bermudez, J.L., 2001, "Frege on Thoughts and Their Structure", *Logical Analysis and History of Philosophy,* 4: 87-105.

Biletzki, A. and A. Matar (eds.), 1998, *The Story of Analytic Philosophy*, New York: Routledge.

Bilgrami, A., 1998, "Why Holism Is Harmless and Necessary", *Philosophical Perspectives, 12: Language, Mind and Ontology,* ed. J.E. Tomberlin, pp. 105-26.

Binkley, T., 1971, "On Reading Investigation § 43", *Philosophy and Phenomenological Research*, 31(3): 429-32.

Bird, G.H., 1961, "Analytic and Synthetic", *The Philosophical Quarterly*, 11(44): 227-37.

Black, C., 1974, "Philosophical Investigations Remark 43 Revisited", *Mind*, 83(332): 596-98.

Black, M., 1934, "The Principle of Verifiability", *Analysis*, 2(1/2): 1-6.

——, 1949, "Carnap's Semantics", *Philosophical Review*, 58(3): 257-64.

——, 1986, "Wittgenstein's Language-games", in *Ludwig Wittgenstein: Critical Assessment*, ed. S. Shanker, vol. II, London: Croom Helm.

Bogen, J., 1972, *Wittgenstein's Philosophy of Language: Some Aspects of Development*, London: Routledge and Kegan Paul.

Boghossian, P.A., 1994, "The Transparency of Mental Content", *Philosophical Perspectives: Logic and Language*, vol. 8, pp. 33-50.

Boisvert, D.R., 1999, "The Trouble with Harrison's 'The Trouble with Tarski'", *The Philosophical Quarterly*, 49(196): 376-83.

Boodin, J.E., 1910, "Truth and Its Object", *The Journal of Philosophy, Psychology and Scientific Methods*, 7(19): 508-21.

Braithwaite, R.B., 1937-38, "Two Ways of Definition by Verification", *Erkenntnis*, 7(1): 281-87.

Brown, R. and J., Watling, 1950-51, "Amending the Verification Principle", *Analysis*, 11(4): 87-89.

Buchler, J., 1937, "Value-Statements", *Analysis*, 4(4): 49-58.

Butchvarov, P., 1960, "Meaning-as-Use and Meaning-as-Correspondence", *Philosophy*, 35(135): 314-25.

Candlish, S., 1999, "A Prolegomenon to an Identity Theory of Truth", *Philosophy*, 74: 199-220.

Cannavo, S., 1965, "On the Verifiability of Universal Empirical Statements", *Analysis*, 26(1): 21-25.

Carl, W., 1994, *Frege's Theory of Sense and Reference: Its Origins and Scope*, New York: Cambridge University Press.

Carnap, R., 1937, *The Logical Syntax of Language,* New York: Harcourt.

——, 1947, *Meaning and Necessity*, Chicago: University of Chicago Press.

——, 1950, *Logical Foundations of Philosophy*, Chicago: University of Chicago Press.

——, 1952, "Empiricism, Semantics and Ontology", in *Semantics and the Philosophy of Language*, ed. L. Linsk, Urbana: University of Illinois Press.

——, 1953, "Testability and Meaning", in *Classics of Analytic Philosophy*, ed. R.R. Ammerman, Bombay: McGraw-Hill.

——, 1981, "Ethics", in *Essential Readings in Logical Positivism,* ed. O. Hanfling, Oxford: Basil Blackwell.

Caton, C.E., 1962, "An Apparent Difficulty in Frege's Ontology", *The Philosophical Review*, 71: 462-75.

Chakraborty, N.N., 2004, *Pursuit of Meaning*, Kolkata: New Age Publishers.

Cooper, D.E., 1973, *Philosophy and the Nature of Language*, London: Logman.

Cunningham, G.W., 1938, "Meaning, Reference and Significance", *Philosophical Review*, 47(2): 155-75.

Currie, G., 1980, "Frege on Thoughts", *Mind* 89(354): 247.

——, 1985, "The Analysis of Thoughts", *The Australasian Journal of Philosophy*, 63: 283-98.

Daitz, E., 1966, "The Picture Theory of Meaning", in *Essay in Conceptual Analysis*, ed. A. Flew, New York: St Martin's Press and Macmillan.

Daniels, C.B., 1988, "Privacy and Verification", *Analysis*, 48(2): 100-02.

Dasgupta, A., 1999, "Language and the Metaphysics of Interpretation: A Critical Note on Davidson's Agenda on Realism", *Indian Philosophical Quarterly*, XXVI(3): 299-324.

David, B., 1979, *Frege's Theory of Judgment*, Oxford: Clarendon Press.

Davidson, D., 1980, *Essays on Actions and Events,* Oxford: Clarendon Press.

——, 1984, *Inquiries into Truth and Interpretation*, Oxford: Clarendon Press.

——, 1984a, "Radical Interpretation", in *Inquiries into Truth and Interpretation*, Oxford: Clarendon Press, pp. 125-39.

——, 1984b, "The Method of Truth in Metaphysics", *Inquiries into Truth and Interpretation,* Oxford: Clarendon Press.

——, 1984c, "Thought and Talk", *Inquiries into Truth and Interpretation,* Oxford: Clarendon Press.

——, 1984d, "Truth and Meaning", *Inquiries into Truth and Interpretation,* Oxford: Clarendon Press.

——, 1990, "The Structure and Content of Truth", *Journal of Philosophy,* 87(6): 279-328.

——, 2001, *Subjective, Intersubjective and Objective,* Oxford: Clarendon Press.

Davidson, D. and J. Hintrikka (eds.), 1975, *Words and Objections: Essays on the Work of W.V. Quine*, London/Boston: D. Reidel.

Devitt, M., 1993, "A Critique of the Case for Semantic Holism", *Philosophical Perspectives*, 7: 281-306.

Dilman, I., 1984, *Quine on Ontology, Necessity and Experience: A Philosophical Critique*, London: Macmillan.

Ducasse, C.J., 1936, "Verification, Verifiability and Meaningfulness", *Journal of Philosophy*, 33(9): 230-63.

——, 1941, "Truth, Verifiability and Propositions about the Future", *Philosophy of Science*, 8(3): 329-37.

Dudman, V.H., 1969, "A Note on Frege on Sense", *The Australasian Journal of Philosophy*, 47: 199-22.

——, 1970, "Frege's Judgment-Stroke", *The Philosophical Quarterly*, 20: 150-62.

——, 1972, "Frege on Assertion", *The Philosophical Quarterly*, 22: 61-64.

Duhem, P., 1962, *The Aim and Structure of Physical Theory*, tr. P.L. Broglie, New York: Athenaeum Publication.

Dummet, M., 1955, "Frege on Functions: A Reply", *The Philosophical Review*, 64: 96-107.

——, 1973, *Frege: Philosophy of Language*, London: Duckworth.

——, 1975, "What Is a Theory of Meaning?", in *Mind and Language*, ed. S. Guttenplan, Cambridge: Cambridge University Press.

——, 1981, *The Interpretation of Frege's Philosophy*, London: Duckworth.

——, 1991a, *Frege and Other Philosophers*, Oxford: Oxford University Press.

——, 1991b, *Frege: Philosophy of Mathematics*, London: Duckworth.

——, 1993, *The Seas of Language*, Oxford/New York: Clarendon Press.

Early Big Typescript (1932) (TS, 211): A typescript composed from volumes VI-X, *Manuscripts,* vol. II, written between 2 February 1929 and 1944.

Esfeld, M., 1998, "Holism and Analytic Philosophy", *Mind*, 107: 365-80.

——, 2001, *Holism in Philosophy of Mind and Philosophy of Physics*, Synthese Library, vol. 298, London: Kluwer Academic Publishers.

Evans, J.L., 1953, "On Meaning and Verification", *Mind*, 62(245): 1-19.

——, 1961, "Meaning and Use", *Philosophy and Phenomenological Research*, 22(2): 251-61.

Evnine, S., 1991, *Donald Davidson*, Cambridge: Polity Press.

Ewing, A.C., 1937, "Meaninglessness", *Mind*, 46(183): 347-64.

Feuer, L.S., 1951, "The Paradox of Verifiability", *Philosophy and Phenomenological Research*, 12(1): 24-41.

Field, H., 1972, "Tarski's Theory of Truth", *Journal of Philosophy*, LXIX(13): 347-75.

——, 1977, "Logic, Meaning and Conceptual Role", *Journal of Philosophy*, 74(7): 347-75.

Fisk, M., 1963, "A Paradox in Frege's Semantics", *Philosophical Studies*, 14: 56-63.

Flew, A. (ed.), 1951 (First Series), *Logic and Language*, Oxford: Basil Blackwell.

Fodor, J. and E. Lepore (eds.), 1992, *Holism: A Shopper's Guide*, Oxford: Blackwell.

Frege, G., 1892, "On Sense and Reference", in *Translations from the Philosophical Writings of Gottlob Frege*, ed. P. Geach and M. Black, 1952, Oxford: Basil Blackwell.

——, 1906, "A Brief Survey of My Logical Doctrines", *Posthumous Writings*, tr. P. Long and ed. R. White 1979, Oxford: Basil Blackwell.

——, 1914, "Logic in Mathematics", in *Posthumous Writings*, tr. P. Loud and ed. R. White, 1979, Oxford: Basil Blackwell.

——, 1915, "My Basic Logical Insights", in *Posthumous Writings*, tr. P. Loud and ed. R. White, 1979, Oxford: Basil Blackwell.

——, 1948, "Sense and Reference", *The Philosophical Review*, 57(3): 209-30.

——, 1952, "On Sense and Meaning", in *Translation from the Philosophical Writings of Gottlob Frege*, ed. M. Black and P. Geach, Oxford: Basil Blackwell.

——, 1956, "The Thought: A Logical Inquiry", *Mind*, 65: 289-311.

——, 1977, "Thoughts", in *Logical Investigations*, ed. P.T. Geach, Oxford: Basil Blackwell.

——, 1979, *Posthumous Writings*, tr. P. Long and ed. R. White, Oxford: Blackwell.

——, 1980, *The Foundations of Arithmetic*, tr. J.L. Austin, Illinois: North Western University Press.

——, 1984, "Compound Thoughts", in *Collected Papers on Mathematics, Logic and Philosophy*, ed. B. McGuinness and tr. M. Black, Oxford: Blackwell.

——, 1997a, *Logical Investigations*, Oxford: Basil Blackwell.

——, 1997b, *The Frege Reader*, ed. M. Beaney, Oxford: Blackwell. Includes tr. of parts of vol. 2 of *Grundgesetze der Aritmetik*.

Friedman, M., 1975, "Physicalism and the Indeterminacy of Translation", *Noûs*, 9(4): 353-74.

——, 1999, *Reconsidering Logical Positivism*, New York: Cambridge University Press.

Fries, H.S., 1936, "On an Empirical Criterion of Meaning", *Philosophy of Science*, 3(2): 143-51.

Gahringer, R.E., 1963, "Analytic Propositions and Philosophical Truths", *The Journal of Philosophy*, 60(17): 481-502.

Gamut, L.T.F., 1991, *Logic, Language and Meaning*, vol. II, London: University of Chicago Press.

Garver, N., 1971, "The Variability of the Analytic", *Philosophy and Phenomenological Research*, 31(3): 409-14.

Gateth, E. and M. John, 1977, *Truth and Meaning*, London: Oxford University Press.

Geach, P.T., 1955, "Class and Concepts", *The Philosophical Review*, 64: 561-70.

Geach, P.T. and M. Black, 1952, *Translations from the Philosophical Writings of Gottlob Frege*, Oxford: Basil Blackwell.

Genova, J., 1995, *Wittgenstein: A Ways of Seeing*, New York: Routledge.

George, A., 1977, "Has Dummett Oversalted His Frege?: Remarks on the Conveyability of Thought", in *Language, Thought and Logic*, ed. R. Heck, Oxford: Oxford University Press, pp. 35-70.

Gibson, R.F. (ed.), 2004, *The Cambridge Companion to Quine*, London: Cambridge University Press.

Glock, H., 2003, *Quine and Davidson on Language, Thought and Reality*, Cambridge: Cambridge University Press.

Glock, H. and L. Arrington (eds.), 1996, *Wittgenstein and Quine*, London: Routledge.

Gluer, K. and Pagin, P., 2003, "Meaning Theory and Autistic Speakers", *Mind and Language*, 18: 23-51.

Gomperz, H., 1941, "The Meanings of 'Meaning'", *Philosophy of Science*, 8(2): 157-83.

Grandy, R., 1973, "Reference, Meaning, and Belief", *The Journal of Philosophy*, 70(14): 439-52.

Grunbaum, A., 1962, "The Falsifiability of Theories: Total or Partial ?", *Synthese*, XIV(1): 17-34.

Guttenplan, S., 1974, *Mind and Language*, Oxford: Clarendon Press.

—— (ed.), 1975, "Thought and Talk", in *Mind and Language*, Oxford: Oxford University Press.

Hacking, I.N., 1975, *Why Does Language Matter to Philosophy?*, Cambridge: Cambridge University Press.

Hahn, L.E. (ed.), 1999, *The Philosophy of Donald Davidson*, Library of Living Philosophers XXVII, Chicago: Open Court Press.

Hale, B. and C. Wright (eds.), 1999, *A Companion to Philosophy of Language*, UK: Basil Blackwell.

Hale, J., 2000, "Radical Interpretation", in *A Companion to the Philosophy of Language*, ed. B. Hale and C. Wright, Oxford: Blackwell, pp. 175-96.

Hanfling, O. (ed.), 1972, *Fundamental Problems in Philosophy*, Bristol: Basil Blackwell in association with The Open University Press.

——, 1981a, *Essential Readings in Logical Positivism*, Oxford: Basil Blackwell.

——, 1981b, *Logical Positivism*, Oxford: Basil Blackwell.

Harman, G., 1968, "Three Levels of Meaning", *The Journal of Philosophy*, 19: 590-602.

——, 1982, "Conceptual Role Semantics", *Notre Dame Journal of Formal Logic*, 23: 242-56.

——, 1987, "Conceptual Role Semantics", in *New Directions in Semantics*, ed. E. Lepore, London: Academic Press.

Healey, R., 1991, "Holism and Non-Separability", *Journal of Philosophy*, 88(8): 393-421.

Heck Jr., R.G., 1997, "Tarski, Truth, and Semantics", *The Philosophical Review*, 106(4): 533-54.

Heck, R., 1985, "The Sense of Communication", *Mind*, 104: 79-106.

Hempel, C., 1935a, "On the Logical Positivists' Theory of Truth", *Analysis*, 2(4): 49-59.

——, 1935b, "Some Remarks on 'Facts' and Proposition", *Analysis*, 3(6): 93-96.

——, 1965, "Problems and Changes in the Empiricist Criterion of Meaning", in *Classics of Analytic Philosophy*, ed. R. Ammerman, New Delhi: McGraw-Hill.

Henrich, D. (ed.), 1983, "A Coherence Theory of Truth and Knowledge", *Kant Order Hegel?*, London, Stuttgart: Klett-Cotta.

Hervey, H., 1961, "The Problem of the Model Language-Game in Wittgenstein's Later Philosophy", *Philosophy*, 36(138): 333-51.

Hinman, L.M., 1983, "Can a Form of Life Be Wrong?", *Philosophy*, 58(225): 339-51.

Hodes, H.T., 1982, "The Composition of Fregean Thoughts", *Philosophical Studies*, 41: 161-78.

Hookway, C., 1987, *Quine*, Oxford: Polity Press.

Hornstein, N., 1982, "Foundationalism and Quine's Indeterminacy of Translation Thesis", *Social Research*, 49: 32-67.

Horwich, P., 1995, "Meaning, Use and Truth: On Whether a Use-Theory of Meaning Is Precluded by the Requirement that Whatever Constitutes the Meaning of Predicate Be Capable of Determining the Set of Things of Which the Predicate Is True and to Which It Ought to be Applied", *Mind*, 104(414): 355-68.

Hospers, J., 1967, *An Introduction to Philosophical Analysis*, London: Prentice-Hall.

Hudson, W.D., 1978, "Language-Games and Presuppositions", *Philosophy*, 53(203): 94-99.

Humphries, B.M., 1970, "Indeterminacy of Translation and Theory", *The Journal of Philosophy*, 67(6): 167-78.

Hunter, J.F.M., 1980, "Wittgenstein on Language and Games", *Philosophy*, 55(213): 293-302.

Izard, C.E., 1969, *The Face of Emotions*, New York: Appleton-Century-Crofts.

Jaggar, A., 1973, "One of the Reasons for the Indeterminacy of Translation", *Philosophy and Phenomenological Research*, 34(2): 257-65.

Jnr, H. and G. Richard (eds.), 1997, *Language, Thought and Logic*, Oxford: Oxford University Press.

Juhosvon, B., 1936-37, "The Truth of Empirical Statement", *Analysis*, 4(5): 65-70.

——, 1937, "Principles of Logical Empiricism", *Mind*, 46(183): 320-46.

Kaufman, A.S., 1953, "The Analytic and the Synthetic: A Tenable Dualism", *The Philosophical Review*, 62(3): 421-26.

Kemp, G., 1995, "Truth in Frege's Laws of Truth", *Synthese*, 105: 31-51.

Kenny, A., 1973, *Wittgenstein*, New York: Penguin Press.

—— (ed.), 1994, *The Wittgenstein Reader*, Cambridge: Blackwell.

Keuth, H., 1978, "Tarski's Definition of Truth and the Correspondence

Theory", *Philosophy of Science*, 45(3): 420-30.

Kirk, R., 1977, "More on Quine's Reasons for Indeterminacy of Translation", *Analysis*, 37(3): 136-41.

——, 1985, "Davidson and Indeterminacy of Translation", *Analysis*, 45(1): 20-24.

Kolbel, M., 2001, "Two Dogmas of Davidsonian Semantics", *The Journal of Philosophy*, 98(12): 613-35.

Kotatko, P. and A. Orenstein (eds.), 2000, *Knowledge, Language and Logic: Questions for Quine*, London: Kluwer.

Kotatko, P. and G. Segal (eds.), 2001, *Interpreting Davidson*, Stanford: CSLI.

Kukla, A. and R. Kukla, 1989, "Meaning Holism and Intentional Psychology", *Analysis*, 49(4): 173-75.

Ladislav, T., 1996, *Problems of Semantics*, London: D. Reidel.

Langer, K.S., 1948, *Philosophy in a New Key*, New York: New American Library Press.

Lazerowitz, M., 1937, "The Principle of Verifiability", *Mind*, 46(183): 372-78.

——, 1939, "Strong and Weak Verification", *Mind*, 48(190): 202-13.

——, 1955, *The Structure of Metaphysics*, London: Routledge.

Lepley, R., 1938, "The Verifiability of Facts and Values", *Philosophy of Science*, 5(3): 310-20.

——, 1940, "The Verifiability of Different Kinds of Facts and Values" *Philosophy of Science*, 7(4): 464-75.

Lepore, E. (ed.), 1986, *Truth and Interpretation: Perspectives on the Philosophy of Donald Davidson*, Oxford: Basil Blackwell.

Levi, A.W., 1964, "Wittgenstein as Dialectician", *The Journal of Philosophy*, 61(4): 127-39.

Levison, A.B., 1965, "Logic, Language, and Consistency in Tarski's Theory of Truth", *Philosophy and Phenomenological Research*, 25(3): 384-92.

Lewis, J., 1988, "Schlick's Critique of Positivism", *PSA: Proceedings of the Biennial Meeting of the Philosophy of Science Association*, vol. 1: *Contributed Papers*, pp. 110-11.

Lewy, C., 1938, "A Note on Empirical Propositions", *Analysis*, 5(3/4): 51-55.

Lindley, T.F., 1964, "'True' and 'False'", *The Journal of Philosophy*, 61(13): 387-95.

Loar, B., 1981, *Mind and Meaning*, Cambridge: Cambridge University Press.

Loewar, B. and G. Rey (ed.), 1991, *Meaning in Mind*, Oxford: Blackwell.

Lormand, E., 1996, "How to Be a Meaning Holist", *Journal of Philosophy*, XCIII(2): 51-73.

Ludwig, K., 1999, "Theories of Meaning, Truth and Interpretation", in *Donald Davidson: Truth, Meaning and Knowledge*, ed. U.M. Zeglen, London: Routledge.

Malcolm, N., 1986, *Nothing Is Hidden: Wittgenstein's Criticism of His Early Thought*, New York: Basil Blackwell.

Malpas, J.E., 1991, "Holism and Indeterminacy", *Dialectica*, 45: 47-58.

——, 1992, *Donald Davidson and the Mirror of Meaning*, Cambridge: Cambridge University Press.

Margolis, E. and S. Laurence, 1998, "Multiple Meanings and the Stability of Content", *The Journal of Philosophy*, 95(5): 255-63.

Marshall, W., 1953, "Frege's Theory of Functions and Objects", *The Philosophical Review*, 62: 374-90.

——, 1956, "Sense and Reference: A Reply", *The Philosophical Review*, 65: 342-61.

Martin, R.M., 1951, "On Tarski's Semantic Conception of Truth", *Philosophy and Phenomenological Research*, 11(3): 411-12.

——, 1952, "On 'Analytic", *Philosophical Studies*, 3: 42-47.

Mauws, M.K. and N. Phillips, 1995, "Understanding Language Games", *Organization Science*, 6(3): 322-34.

McDonald, M., 1936, "Language and Reference", *Analysis*, 4(2/3): 33-41.

McDonough, R., 1989, "Towards a Non-Mechanistic Theory of Meaning", *Mind*, 98(389): 1-21.

McDowell, J., 1980, "Meaning, Communication and Knowledge", in *Philosophical Subjects: Essays Presented to P.F. Strawson*, ed. Z.V. Straaten, Oxford: Oxford University Press.

McDowell, J. and G. Evans, 1976, *Truth and Meaning*, London: Oxford University Press.

Miller, A., 1998, *Philosophy of Language*, New York: Routledge.

Miller, D.L., 1943, "Meaning and Verification", *The Philosophical Review*, 52(6): 604-09.

Moore, G.E., 1959, *Philosophical Papers*, New York: Allen and Unwin.

Morris, K.J., 1994, "The 'Context Principle' in the Later Wittgenstein", *The Philosophical Quarterly*, 44(176): 294-310.

Moulines, C., 1986, "The Ways of Holism", *Noûs*, 20(3): 313-32.

Mulhall, S., 1987, "Davidson on Interpretation and Understanding", *The Philosophical Quarterly*, 37(148): 319-22.

Munitz, M.K., 1981, *Contemporary Analytic Philosophy*, New York: Macmillan.

Nagel, E., 1934, "Verifiability, Truth and Verification", *The Journal of Philosophy*, 31(6): 141-48.

Noonan, H.W., 2001, *Frege: A Critical Introduction*, Cambridge: Polity Press.

O'Connor, D.J., 1950, "Some Consequences of Professor A.J. Ayer's Verification Principle", *Analysis*, 10(3): 67-72.

Orenstein, A. and P. Kotatko (eds.), 2000, *Knowledge, Language and Logic: Questions for Quine*, London: Kluwer Academic Publishers.

Palmer, A., 1988, "Truth and Meaning", in *Concept and Object*, New York: Routledge.

Parkinson, G.H.R., 1988, *An Encyclopaedia of Philosophy*, London: Routledge.

Pasch, A., 1956, "Empiricism: One 'Dogma' or Two", *The Journal of Philosophy*, 53(9): 302-11.

Passmore, J., 1957, *A Hundred Years of Philosophy*, London: Penguin.

Patt, J.B., 1907, "Truth and Its Verification", *The Journal of Philosophy, Psychology and Scientific Methods*, 4(12): 320-24.

Peacocke, C., 1979, *Holistic Explanation: Action, Space, Interpretation*, Oxford: Clarendon Press.

——, 1999, "Holism", in *A Companion to the Philosophy of Language*, ed. B. Hale and C. Wright, UK: Blackwell, pp. 331-68.

Pears, D.F. and B.F. McGuinness (eds.), 1961, *Tractatus Logico-Philosophicus*, London: Routledge and Kegan Paul.

Penco, C., 2002, "Holism, Strawberries and Hairdryers", *Topoi*, 21(1-2): 47-54.

Perry, J., 1977, "Frege on Demonstratives", *The Philosophical Review*, 86: 474-97.

Phillips, D.Z. and P. Winch (eds.), 1989, *Wittgenstein: Attention to Particulars*, London: Macmillan.

Pitcher, G., 1972, *The Philosophy of Wittgenstein*, New Delhi: Prentice Hall of India.

Platts, M., 1979, *Ways of Meaning*, London: Routledge.

Pompa, L., 1968, "Family Resemblance: A Reply", *The Philosophical Quarterly*, 18(73): 347-53.

Post, H., 1975, "The Problem of Atomism", *The British Journal for the Philosophy of Science*, 26(1): 19-26.

Pradhan, R.C., 1996, *Philosophy of Meaning and Representation*, New Delhi: D.K. Printworld.

——, 2002, *The Great Mirror: An Essay on Wittgenstein's Tractatus*, New Delhi: Kalki Prakash.

Proto-Philosophical Investigations (TS, 220): A typescript of the first half of the pre-war version of the *Philosophical Investigations.*

Putnam, H., 1974, "The Refutation of Conventionalism", *Noûs*, VIII(1): 25-40.

——, 1986, "Meaning Holism", in *The Philosophy of W.V. Quine*, ed. L. Hahn and P. Schilpp, La Salle, IL: Open Court.

Quine, W.V., 1960a, "Carnap and Logical Truth", *Synthese*, 12(4): 350-74.

——, 1960b, *Word and Object*, Massachusetts: The MIT Press.

——, 1961a, "Two Dogmas of Empiricism", in *From a Logical Point of View*, Cambridge, MA: Harvard University Press.

——, 1961b, *From a Logical Point of View*, New York: Harper Torchbooks.

——, 1964, "Meaning and Translation", in *The Structure of Language: Readings in the Philosophy of Language*, ed. J.A. Fodor and J. Katz, London: Prentice-Hall, pp. 460-78.

——, 1969, *Ontological Relativity and Other Essays*, Cambridge: Cambridge University Press.

——, 1970, "On the Reasons for the Indeterminacy of Translation", *The Journal of Philosophy*, 67(6): 178-83.

——, 1972a, "Meaning and Truth", in *Fundamental Problems in Philosophy*, ed. O. Hanfling, Bristol: Basil Blackwell in association with The Open University Press, pp. 287-302.

——, 1972b, "On Carnap's Views on Ontology", in *New Readings in Philosophical Analysis*, ed. H. Feigl, W. Sellars and K. Lehrer, New York: Meredith Corporation, pp. 597-601.

——, 1976, *The Ways of Paradox and Other Essays*, London: Harvard University Press.

——, 1981, *Theories and Things*, London: The Belknap Press of Harvard University Press.

——, 1986, "Reply to H. Putnam", in *The Philosophy of W.V. Quine*, ed. P. Schillp, Illinois: Open Court.

——, 1987a, *Quiddities*, Cambridge: The Belknap Press of Harvard University Press.

——, 1987b, "Indeterminacy of Translation Again", *The Journal of Philosophy*, 84(1): 5-10.

——, 1990, *Pursuit of Truth*, Cambridge, MA: Harvard University Press.

Quine, W.V. and J.S. Ullian, 1978, *The Web of Belief*, New York: Random House Publication.

Ramberg, B.T., 1984, *Donald Davidson's Philosophy of Language: An Introduction*, New York: Basil Blackwell.

Rhees, R. (ed.), 1974, *Philosophical Grammar*, tr. A.J.P. Kenny, Oxford: Blackwell.

——, 1975, *Philosophical Remarks*, tr. R. Hargreaves and R. White, Oxford: Blackwell.

——, 1976, *Cause and Effect: Intuitive Awareness*, tr. P. Winch, *Philosophia*, 6: 3-4.

Rhees, R. and G.E.M. Anscombe (eds.), 1958, *Philosophical Investigation*, tr. G.E.M. Anscombe, 2nd edn, Oxford: Blackwell.

Ricketts, T., 1985, "Frege the Tractatus, and the Logocentric Predicament", *Noŭs*, 9: 3-15.

Roger F. Gibson, Jr. (ed.), 2004, *Quintessence: Basic Readings from the Philosophy of W.V. Quine*, London: The Belknap Press of Harvard University Press.

Rorty, R. (ed.), 1967, "Systematically Misleading Expressions", in *The Linguistic Turn*, Chicago: Chicago University Press.

——, 1972, "Indeterminacy of Translation and of Truth", *Synthese*, XXIII(4): 443-62.

Russell, Bertrand, 1965, "Descriptions", in *Classics of Analytic Philosophy*, ed. Robert R. Ammermann, New Delhi: Tata McGraw-Hill.

Ruja, H., 1961, "The Present Status of the Verifiability Criterion", *Philosophy and Phenomenological Research*, 22(2): 216-22.

Ryle, G., 1936-37, "Unverifiability-by-Me", *Analysis*, 4(1): 1-11.

Sankey, H., 1991, "Incommensurability, Translation and Understanding", *The Philosophical Quarterly*, 41(165): 414-26.

Savery, W., 1938, "The Synoptic Theory of Truth", *The Philosophical Review*, 47(4): 347-74.

Schlick, M., 1979, *Philosophical Papers*, London: Dordrecht Publication.

——, 1981, "Meaning and Verification", in *Essential Readings in Logical Positivism*, ed. by O. Hanfling, Oxford: Basil Blackwell.

Schulte, J., 2004, "The Builders' Language: The Opening Sections", in *Wittgenstein at Work: Method in the Philosophical Investigations*, ed. E. Ammereller and E. Fischer, London: Routledge.

Searle, J.R., 1957, "Russell's Objections to Frege's Theory of Sense and Reference", *Analysis*, 18: 137-43.

Sen, P.K., 1991, *Reference and Truth*, New Delhi: ICPR.

Sengupta, Kalyan 1969, *Language and Philosophy*, Bombay: Allied Publishers.

Shanker, S. (ed.), 1986, *Ludwig Wittgenstein: Critical Assessments*, vol. 1, London: Croom Helm.

Sidgwick, A., 1936, "Verifiability and Meaning", *Mind*, 45(177): 61-66.

Preyer, Gerhard, Frank Siebelt and Alexander Ulfig (eds.), 1994, *Language, Mind and Epistemology*, Dordrecht: Kluwer.

Simons, P., 1987, *Parts: A Study in Ontology*, Oxford: Clarendon Press.

Sinisi, V.F., 1967, "Tarski on the Inconsistency of Colloquial Language",

Philosophy and Phenomenological Research, 27(4): 537-41.

Sluga, H. and D. Stern (eds.), 1996, *The Cambridge Companion to Wittgenstein*, New York: Cambridge University Press.

Soames, S., 1984, "What Is a Theory of Truth?", *The Journal of Philosophy*, 81(8): 411-29.

——, 2003, *Philosophical Analysis in the Twentieth Century*, vol. 2, Princeton/ Oxford: Princeton University Press.

Solomon, M., 1989, "Quine's Point of View", *The Journal of Philosophy*, 86(3): 113-36.

Stace, W.T., 1935, "Metaphysics and Meaning", *Mind*, 44(176): 417-38.

——, 1947a, "Positivism", *Mind*, 53(211): 215-37.

——, 1947b, "Are All Empirical Statements Hypotheses?", *The Journal of Philosophy*, 44(2): 29-38.

Stirton, W.R., 1997, "Anti-Realism, Truth-Conditions and Verificationism", *Mind*, 106(424): 697-716.

Stjernberg, F., 1991, *The Public Nature of Meaning*, Stockholm: Almquist and Wiksell.

Stoecker, R. (ed.), 1993, *Reflecting Davidson*, Berlin: W. de Gruyter.

Suppes, P., 1988, "Philosophical Implications of Tarski's Work", *The Journal of Symbolic Logic*, 53(1): 80-91.

Talmage, C.J.L. and Mercer, M., 1991, "Meaning Holism and Interpretability", *The Philosophical Quarterly*, 41(164): 301-15.

Tarski, A., 1956, "The Concept of Truth in Formalized Languages", in *Logic, Semantics, Mathematics*, Oxford: Clarendon Press.

The Big Typescript (1933) (TS, 213): A rearrangement, with modifications, written additions and deletions, of EBT.

Thompkins, E.F., 1990, "A Farewell to Forms of Life", *Philosophy*, 65(252): 181-97.

Tugendhat, E., 1970, "The Meaning of 'Bedeutung' in Frege", *Analysis*, 30: 177-89.

Urban, W.M., 1937, "Value Propositions and Verifiability", *The Journal of Philosophy*, 34(22): 589-602.

Van Heijenoort, J., 1977a, "Sense in Frege", *Journal of Philosophical Logic*, 6: 93-102.

——, 1977b, "Frege on Sense Identity", *Journal of Philosophical Logic*, 6: 103-08.

Verheggen, C., 2007, "Triangulating with Davidson", *The Philosophical Quarterly*, 57(226): 96-103.

von Wright, G.H., 1967, *Zettel*, tr. G.E.M. Anscombe, Oxford: Blackwell.

——, 1972, *Tractatus Logico-Philosophicus*, tr. G.H. Von Wright, London: Blackwell.

——, 1974a, *Letters to Russell, Keynes and Moore*, ed. G.H. Von Wright, Oxford: Blackwell.

——, 1974b, *Philosophical Grammar*, ed. R. Rhees, tr. A. Kennay, Oxford: Basil Blackwell.

——, 1975, *Philosophical Remarks*, ed. R. Rhees and tr. R. Hargreaves and R. White, Oxford: Basil Blackwell.

——, 1979, *Notebooks 1914-1916*, ed. G.H. Von Wright and G.E.M. Anscombe, tr. G.E.M. Anscombe, Oxford: Basil Blackwell, 2nd edn.

——, 1982, *Wittgenstein*, Oxford: Basil Blackwell.

von Wright, G.H. and G.E.M. Anscombe (eds.), 1961a, *Notebooks 1914-16*, tr. G.E.M. Anscombe, Oxford: Basil Blackwell.

——, 1961b, *Tractatus Logico-Philosophicus*, tr. D.F. Pears and B.F. McGuniess, London: Routledge and Kegan Paul.

von Wright, G.H. and H. Nyman (eds.), 1980, *Remarks on the Philosophy of Psychology*, vol. 1, tr. Luckhardt and M.A.E. Aue, Oxford: Blackwell Publication.

von Wright, G.H., G.E.M. Anscombe and D. Paul (eds.), 1969, *On Certainty*, tr. G.E.M. Anscombe, Oxford: Blackwell.

von Wright, G.H., R. Rhees and G.E.M. Anscombe (eds.), 1978, *Remarks on the Foundation of Mathematics*, tr. G.E.M. Anscombe, Oxford: Blackwell.

Vuillemin, J., 1986, "On Duhem's and Quine Theses", in *The Philosophy of W.V. Quine*, ed. L. Hahn and P. Schilpp, La Salle, IL: Open Court.

Wagner, S.J., 1986, "Quine's Holism", *Analysis*, 46(1): 1-6.

Waismann, F., 1951, *Verifiability, Logic and Language,* ed, A. Flew, vol. 1, Oxford: Basil Blackwell.

——, 1981, "Meaning and Verification", in *Essential Readings in Logical Positivism*, ed. Oswald Hanfling, Oxford: Basil Blackwell Publication.

Waismann, F. and R. Harre (eds.), 1965, *The Principles of Linguistic Philosophy*, London: Macmillan.

——, 1968, "Verifiability", in *The Theory of Meaning*, ed. G.H.R. Parkinson, Oxford: Oxford University Press.

Wang, H., 1985, "Two Commandments of Analytic Empiricism", *The Journal of Philosophy*, 82(9): 449-62.

Weiler, G., 1967, "A Note on Meaning and Use", *Mind*, 76(303): 424-27.

Weinberg, J.K., 1936, *An Examination of Logical Positivism*, London: Routledge.

Werkmeister, W.H., 1937, "Seven Theses of Logical Positivism Critically Examined", *Philosophical Review*, 46(3): 276-97.

White, A.R., 1954, "A Note on Meaning and Verification", *Mind*, 63(249): 66-69.

——, 1970, *Truth*, London: Macmillan.

Whiteley, C.H., 1939, "On Meaning and Verifiability", *Analysis*, 6(5/6): 79-86.

Wiggins, D., 1984, "On the Sense and Reference of Predicate Expressions", *Philosophical Quarterly*, 34: 311-28.

——, 1997, "Meaning and Truth Conditions: From Frege's Grand Design to Davidson", in *A Companion to the Philosophy of Language*, ed. H. Bob and C. Wright, Oxford: Blackwell.

Will, F.L., 1940, "Verifiability and the External World", *Philosophy of Science*, 7(2): 182-91.

Williams, M., 1999, "Meaning and Deflationary Truth", *The Journal of Philosophy*, 96(11): 545-64.

Wisdom, J., 1938, "Metaphysics and Verification", *Mind*, 47(188): 452-98.

——, 1945, "Positivism", *Mind*, 45(213): 65-70.

——, 1963, "Metamorphoses of the Verifiability Theory of Meaning", *Mind*, 72(287): 335-47.

Wittgenstein, L., 1929-1944, *Manuscripts*, vol. II.

——, 1958, *Blue and Brown Book,* Oxford: Blackwell.

——, 2001, *Philosophical Investigations,* London: Blackwell.

Wohlstetter, A., 1936, "The Structure of the Proposition and the Fact", *Philosophy of Science*, 3(2): 167-84.

Wolgast, E., 1987, "Whether Certainty is a Form of Life", *The Philosophical Quarterly*, 37: 151-65.

Zeglen, U.M. (ed.), 1991, *Donald Davidson: Truth, Meaning and Knowledge*, London: Routledge.

Zimmerman, M., 1962, "The Status of Verifiability Principle", *Philosophy and Phenomenological Research*, 22(3): 334-43.

Index